Back From the Edge of Hell

The Autobiography of
Two Time World Heavyweight Champion

Pinklon Thomas

AS TOLD TO

JOHN GREENBURG

DEDICATION

I wish to dedicate this book to the memory of my deceased parents, Pinklon, Sr. and Lorene, my wife, DaJuana, my daughters PaQuana, Peyton, Pierra, and my five grandchildren, Gregrion, Roniqua, Kyah, Irelynn and Liam. They have given me their unconditional love, understanding and empathy on a daily basis.

SERENITY PRAYER

By Reinhold Niebuhr

"God grant me the serenity
to accept the things I cannot change,
courage to change the things I can
and wisdom to know the difference."

PROLOGUE

It was 1986, and television cameras were focused on me as I stood in a boxing ring before a sold-out Vegas crowd. I was about to defend my world heavyweight crown. My promoter was the legendary Don King. I had been guided by Angelo Dundee, who trained my boxing idol, Muhammad Ali. The charismatic Ali, embraced by the world as the greatest fighter of all, was sitting at ringside, cheering me on. The man who inspired me had become my friend. I was being paid eight hundred fifty grand to fight twelve three-minute rounds, an obscene rate of pay for thirty-six minutes of work. To the thousands in the arena and millions seated on couches and La-Z-Boys in front of TV sets and holding their favorite ice cold drinks, I was at the top of a mountain so tall I could almost touch Heaven.

In reality, I was standing at the edge of Hell, and the flames were about to lick at my toes. It was only a matter of time until I would fall into the fiery abyss.

That was thirty years ago, and I'm still here. I was saved only through the Grace of God, and I am so grateful for that. Keeping as many young people as possible from making the same mistakes I made and helping misguided souls find their way out of the dark cave of addiction have become my callings.

This is my story. It may seem rough, rugged, and raw, but is not meant to glorify living fast, living hard or living on the edge. If someone were to offer me twenty million for leading just one young person down the path I took, I would throw every dollar in their face. The road I traveled leads only to despair and doom. I should have died several times but by the Grace of God, I'm alive and determined to help as many as I can turn their lives around, develop a work ethic, start living honorably and find happiness.

The events I describe are all true. Some names have been changed out of privacy considerations.

Pinklon Thomas, Jr.
2016

CONTENTS

I CAME FROM GOOD STOCK

Hindsight can be humbling. When I think of how I squandered the advantages I had growing up, it frightens me. I did not inherit poverty. I was born into a family with high standards, cherished heirlooms and fine traditions to pass along to future generations. I came from good parents who weren't the sort to be looking for handouts or defrauding the system. They worked hard, owned their own home and lived by the Good Book.

My father, Pinklon Thomas, Sr., was an honorable man who was a good husband, a good father, a good citizen, a good neighbor, served his country and worked hard from the time he was a child. His story is worthy of a book. I didn't realize what a great man he was, how much he had to offer and how much I could have learned by listening to him when I was a knuckleheaded kid.

Dad was born May twentieth, 1914 in Eatonton, Georgia, and was the youngest of twenty two children. My grandmother on my father's side was a Native American whose maiden name was Ella "Pinkie" Boswell and Granddad's name was Anderson Thomas. They named my dad "Pinkerton" but he always had trouble spelling and pronouncing his name. A kindly teacher came up with the name "Pinklon," which was easier for him to say and spell. His teacher promised, "No one will ever know what your name really is unless you tell 'em." Dad went along, and the name stuck.

When he was seven, my grandparents moved their family to the Ensly neighborhood of Birmingham, Alabama, and my father went to work in the cotton fields. He labored from sunup to sundown filling a bag that would end up weighing more than he did. He was paid five cents for each pound of cotton picked and did such a good job he was given a raise to a whopping ten cents a pound. He continued picking cotton until he was twenty-one years old

From his earliest years, Dad believed in living the right way and working hard to achieve his dreams. In 1927, when he was thirteen, he accepted the Lord as his Personal Savior at the Shiloh Baptist Church in Ensly. My father got his first hourly wage job in 1935, working in a mine for the Tennessee Coal, Iron and Railroad Company. The company was part of U.S. Steel, owned all the land in Ensley, even the fields where Dad picked cotton, and provided housing for the workers. He dug for coal ten hours a day, six days a week, for twenty-six cents an hour. He and his coworkers replaced convict laborers leased to the company by the state prison system.

He also sang baritone as part of a quartet called The Four Great Wonders. Their showmanship built interest, brought worshipers to their feet and had congregations clapping their hands in time to their harmonizing. The quartet followed "The Gospel Highway," an underground form of show business with performances in churches and at religious gatherings under tents. In recalling those days, Dad said, "The four of us split between fifteen to twenty-five bucks each time we sang. We thought we were well compensated."

Like many African Americans living in the South before World War II, my father was lured north by the promise of great opportunity and migrated to St. Paul, Minnesota in 1941. At the start of the war, he was drafted into the Army. My dad was assigned to be a cook, earned a promotion to mess sergeant and later achieved the rank of technical sergeant.

Leaving the service, he came to Pontiac, Michigan in March, 1942. The wartime economy was in high gear and Pontiac's nine factories operated day and night. With his singing talent and gift for preparing down home ox tails and mouth-watering hams, Dad made friends and picked up two nicknames: "Phil" and "Big Boy." It wasn't that my father had unusual physical size. He was five ten and a hundred seventy pounds in his prime, but was called Big Boy because of his big baritone voice and big heart. He also received compliments for his stylish clothes, and was never without a borsalino hat. It was his trademark.

He met a woman ten years younger than him named Lorene Willie Beard. Her friends and family called her "Rene Bene" (pronounced Reeny Beeny). She became the love of his life, and they married June third, 1944. Mom and dad had two girls named Audrey and Bernice, and then I was born February tenth, 1958, when my dad was forty-three years old. My parents were happily married fifty-eight years. Mom died in 2002 and dad lived to be a hundred, passing away in 2014.

When I was growing up, Pontiac was forty five percent African American, but the south side, where we lived, was ninety eight percent black. My father worked hard, saved his money and purchased our home on Fildew Street for twenty thousand back in the 1950's. Dad held several jobs in order to support our family. He worked for American Forging and Socket Company from 1944 through 1959. He was also employed at Oakland Park and worked as a bus boy for Pearl's Chop Suey and a Howard Johnson restaurant. In addition, he operated a jitney cab and had a large clientele he drove to and from stores and work.

My mother worked as a domestic for wealthy families in Bloomfield Hills and Birmingham, Michigan. In her spare time, she did hair in our kitchen for women who had been coming to her for years. There were so many, our living room served as a waiting area. While Momma used her

3

curling irons and straightening combs to work her magic, her customers would catch up on the latest gossip. She also sold dinners from our house. Her delicious collard greens, barbeque spare ribs, fried chicken, fried catfish and spaghetti dinners attracted people from all over the neighborhood. She cleared at least seventy-five bucks each weekend from her cooking.

Since Dad knew how to dress and took pride in his appearance, he made sure I was well groomed, had nice clothes and knew how to make a good first impression. When I was eleven, Dad bought me a one button suit from an exclusive men's store in Bloomfield Hills costing a hundred twenty-eight dollars. My mother was angry with him for spending so much on an Easter suit. I wore it to school the day our pictures were taken. Walking into the classroom, I immediately captured the attention of my male teacher, who was wearing the same style garment. He asked, "Where'd you get that suit from?"

I proudly replied, "My daddy bought it for me."

Dad was a Baptist for nearly fifty years but in 1970, when I was twelve, he was baptized into the Franklin Road Church of Christ. From then on, Dad hosted weekly Bible studies.

Some of my earliest memories were of Momma taking me and my sisters to church. She always prepared Sunday's dinner on Saturday, so we could eat after returning from the services. They seemed to last forever and there were times I became fidgety and got out of line. Momma wouldn't put up with that. She would take me down to the basement of the church, put me over her knee and give me a sound spanking. When we returned to our pew, my mind was right, and I would often lean over on her lap and fall asleep.

There was music and laughter in our home, with Christmas the crown jewel of our family activities. Mom and Dad tried to make the atmosphere even more fun by starting a family tradition of ice cream and cake birthdays. My father declared, "Not one birthday in this house will be spent with absence of ice cream and cake." Momma always encouraged my participation in school activities and never allowed me to go lacking. One time, she made a Hawaiian shirt for me to wear in a school play. It was as good, if not better, than those sold in stores and drew lots of compliments.

My parents did all they could to raise their children right, and there was deep emotional closeness within our family. During my earliest years, our home was pleasant and comfortable, but I had to endure physical problems. When very small, I was so knock kneed and pigeon toed I couldn't walk properly. My mother rubbed a castor oil mixture on my legs every day and prayed over them, hoping that would solve the problem. My legs straightened out, but I became bowlegged. I was very tall for my age, which kept me from being picked on, but my leg and foot issues prevented my clothes from hanging on me properly. I became determined to do something about it. I made a conscious effort to keep my legs and feet straight whenever I walked, worked hard at it and my legs finally straightened out when I was eleven. Once that happened, I could run very fast and began competing in track. I loved to run and whether racing or chasing or just breaking into a sprint, I moved my feet as fast as I could whenever I had the chance.

When I was seven years old, I was growing at a rapid rate. One afternoon, Dad was sitting in the living room with Robert Jones, a next-door neighbor who was like a second father to me. I heard my dad say, "Ya know, I lost my whole paycheck when Joe Louis fought Max Schmeling the first time and the German beat 'im."

Robert asked, "How much didja lose?"

"Fourteen dollars, a week's pay… lotta money back then." My father added, "When Joe Louis fought Schmeling the second time, he said, 'If ya kill the body, the head will die,' and Joe won. When he fought Billy Conn, he said, 'Ya can run, but ya can't hide,' and Joe won again." Dad and Robert spent an hour discussing great fights and fighters, and I hung on every word.

It was the first time I ever heard my father talk about boxing, and he made it sound so interesting I began to think about trying it. Prior to that, I was intrigued by gangsters in the old James Cagney and Humphrey Bogart movies Momma and I watched while sitting together on a couch in front of the television set. Our shared interest in gangster films helped us bond, and we became best friends. Listening to Dad and Robert Jones opened up a new world to me. I started watching boxing on TV, especially whenever Muhammad Ali appeared. This was about the time the charismatic heavyweight converted to Islam and changed his name from Cassius Clay.

Two months after arousing my interest in the fight game, my father surprised me with a present. He brought home two pairs of boxing gloves. I was physically suited for the sport because Momma made sure I had plenty to eat. She was as good a cook as Dad and in some ways, even better. Whenever she rattled her pots and pans, she performed wizardry in the kitchen and produced delectable dishes. All the good eating helped me become unusually large for my age. My friends started calling me "The Big Kid." When other boys in our neighborhood heard Big Boy had bought boxing gloves for The Big Kid, five of the older ones showed up in our backyard to take me on.

One of them was a mouthy kid named Michael. He was twelve years old, five feet ten inches and a hundred forty. I was seven years old, five foot eight and weighed one twenty-five. He thought he could shuffle, shimmy and talk smack just like Ali. I said to my father, "Daddy, let him be first," so my dad and his pal Robert gloved us up, and the bout began. Michael came at me hard, trying to force me into a corner. When he cornered me, I unloaded with body shots that made him wince and groan. My father shouted, *"Junior! Junior, quit hittin' him to the body!*

Man, you gonna hurt that boy!" He stopped the fight, so I earned a TKO in my very first boxing match.

I heard Robert, say, "Big Boy, that son of yours gonna be a champion someday." It makes me a little sad to recall the moment because Robert Jones wasn't around when I became a champ. He died when I was twelve years old.

Boxing helped bring me out of my shell. I was very timid and shy as a young child. I spoke so softly Momma would often say, "I can't read lips, Junior, talk louder." I became terrified if called on to read aloud in class. My voice was so soft the teacher kept saying, "Speak up, Pinklon, speak up!" and my hands trembled as they held the book.

A profound change occurred when I was eight. I was climbing a rope in a gym class, but lost my grip and fell to the floor. When I woke up, I was home in bed and my head throbbed with fiery pain. My mother walked into my bedroom after hearing me awaken and I said, "Momma, my head hurts."

She replied, "Remember when you were climbin' the rope and fell and hit your head?"

"All I remember is fallin'. How'd I get here?"

"No need to worry 'bout that. Doctor says you should rest a coupla days. Just take it easy. I'll call you when it's time to eat."

I was later told I suffered a concussion. Two days of rest made me feel much better. The headaches went away, but there was a change in my personality. I became a fearless, outspoken, rebellious child who acted impulsively without any thought of the consequences. I transformed from a boy who rarely ventured into challenging situations to one eager to try new things and take chances.

I had become a fearless young boy, but also an impulsive risk taker. When I was in third grade, I skipped school with two older boys; Joey and Alfred. Joey was nine and Alfred was a twelve-year-old petty thief willing to take chances. My mother didn't like Alfred at all and didn't want me hanging around him. He knew it and wouldn't come near my house. I disobeyed and would meet up with him because I thought he knew the score and I felt an indescribable feeling of freedom when I was with him. We lived in the moment without any concern for consequences.

With an entire day to ourselves, I asked Joey and Alfred, "What we gonna do?" Alfred replied, "We gonna have fun. Let's go to Kroger's. I'll show ya somethin."

My twelve-year-old buddy was wearing a long sleeved shirt and trousers way too big for him. Just before we entered the supermarket, Alfred let us in on his plan. "We goin' for cigarettes. Stand around me so's they can't see what I'm doin."

I replied, "Yeah buddy, I'm down for that," and Joey nodded his head.

Cartons of smokes were kept on shelves near checkout lanes, allowing shoppers to make their selections and put them in their carts before checking out. We went to shelves near a vacant checkout lane, and Joey and I shielded Alfred. Quick as a gnat, he slipped an entire carton up his left sleeve. He unhurriedly walked away as calm as could be and didn't arouse any suspicion.

Alfred doubled down by heading for the beer section and once again, Joey and I gave him cover. He slipped four cans of brew up his right sleeve and tucked two more in his waistband. He managed to keep the beer and cigarettes in his sleeves until we made a clean getaway.

We took our stolen goodies to a big open field with a pond in the middle known as Farmer Brown's. It was next to a truck stop, a shopping center and radio station WPON. We sat on a black wooden railing surrounding the pond, smoked, drank two beers each and thought we were the coolest cats alive. The beer made us lightheaded, so we rolled up our pants legs and walked into the pond, singing, "Wade in the water. Wade in the water, children. God's gonna trouble the water."

After two hours of clowning around and pretending to be grownups, Alfred came up with another idiotic idea. "Let's go to Cunningham's

Drug Store!" Following his lead, we entered the store without knowing what he had in mind. Joey and I went to the magazine racks and were immediately approached by an eagle eyed, pasty faced, paunchy male clerk who asked, "What are you two doin'?"

"Lookin' at the magazines," I replied.

"Well, look with your eyes. Don't touch any of 'em."

Joey and I turned away from the reading material and left the store. That was enough time for Alfred to swipe three containers of hair straightening solution and escape unnoticed. From there, the three of used a room with a sink in a Laundromat to put the solution on our hair.

All three of us had wavy pompadours announcing to the world we'd been up to no good. Joey's older brother, Johnny, was first to notice. He ran up to us and said, "I'm gonna tell Daddy and Rene (meaning my mother) what you done."

Alfred shook the spot and abandoned us. I knew I was in for some terrible punishment, but wasn't sure what it would be. I thought, *Why did we hafta change our hair? That was stupid! People gonna wonder where we got the hair stuff.*

I hated the thought of going home, but knew there was no way out of it. When I walked in, Momma was still at work, so I went to my room and agonized over what was about to come my way. My mother received a phone call from Joey's dad shortly after she came home and he filled her in on what the three of us had done. She walked into my room and got right on my case by saying, "Take off your pants."

While I was getting them off, she went to the trees and bushes not far from our backdoor, broke off some switches and removed the leaves. She wore my butt out with the switches. It went on all throughout the house because I kept trying to run from her. She was spry enough to catch me, hold me by an arm and keep whipping me. When she finally stopped, my backside was on fire, but I thought, *Good, that's over with.*

I started to go to my bedroom, but Momma said, "Not so fast."

She sat me down on a stool in the kitchen and said, "I'm gonna make sure you won't be wearin' any of that stuff on your head." Using electric clippers, she cut off all my hair. I was bald as a cue ball.

When Dad got home, Momma told him what happened. He said, "Junior, you know that ain't right." He didn't punish me anymore because Momma was the disciplinarian in our family.

After receiving a dose of "Act Right" from my mother, I stopped hanging out with Alfred *and* Joey. I was too young to be bald headed and liked my hair more than I liked Joey. As for Alfred, I knew he wouldn't do me any good and was headed to less than nowhere. He continued as a petty thief until he was eighteen, when he was sent to prison for the first time. All prison did was turn him into a hardened criminal committing more serious offenses. His bad deeds caught up with him, as it does with all criminals. Today, he's serving a life sentence in a Michigan prison, waiting for death and welcoming Hell like an old friend.

WINE AND WEED LEAD ME TO HEROIN

Boxing and gangsters weren't my only interests. I inherited a good, strong baritone voice from my father and once I lost my shyness, loved to sing. At ten, I began hanging around with guys four and five years older who were impressed with my talent. The oldest was Johnny, a kid whose father worked as a postal clerk and mother was seldom at home. His house became our hang out. Johnny had a cassette recorder and microphone, and we would record our versions of Motown hits. We felt destined to become big stars, but were legends in our own minds. Our jam sessions introduced me to the joys of wine. We lubricated our vocal chords with "joy juice," putting away bottles of Ripple, Bali Hai and Boone's Farm. It was fun getting tipsy and being part of a group of older guys. There didn't seem to be any harm in it, but it was a first step down the wrong path.

A year later, when I was eleven, I began running track. This introduced me to two people who had profound effects on my life; one positive, the other negative. The good influence was Bob Kaiser, who became my coach and lifelong friend. The bad influence was Lorenzo Richardson, a fifteen-year-old track athlete known as Slim, who turned me on to weed. I tried to get Johnny and others I sang with interested in pot, but they'd rather stick to their wine. For me, marijuana made me unafraid to try other things that would get me high.

Slim and I went from weed to "mixed jive," low grade heroin diluted with quinine. It was sold in rolled up aluminum foil, and each package cost ten dollars. We scooped it out using plastic coffee stirrers from McDonald's. The stirrers had the famous Golden Arches at one end and a scooper holding precisely one hundred milligrams at the other. Snorting mixed jive made me feel happy, mellow as a cello and free from the cares of the world. I was fortunate not to experience side effects.

We'd snort mixed jive off album covers and got high listening to Miles Davis and other jazz greats. The guys Slim and I used it with were much older than us. Some were in their early twenties. Being accepted by an older, "cooler" group made me feel special. Boys my age seemed like dumb little kids who weren't at my level. I thought I was way ahead of them, but was really falling behind and showing no more brain power than a wet paper towel.

I was blessed to have great relationships with both my sisters. Audrey was the oldest and, in some ways, was a second mother for me. She was always supportive, was kind and was there for me whether I did right or wrong. I could talk to her about anything and many of her friends, both male and female, became my friends. Audrey never judged me and at times when I was high, she would cover for me until I sobered up.

Mixed jive cost money, and I supported my habit by selling weed to kids at school. I made more than needed to pay for what I was using and felt like I was becoming a big man, when I was actually turning into a junkie and creating a mental maze for myself I might never solve. I was living in an imaginary world of guns, music, rarified fashion and fast money seen on TV and in movies. I was so enthralled with the street scenes and hustler schemes in Superfly, I paid to see it five times. I wanted to be just like "Priest," the character played by Ron O'Neal; the way he walked, the way he dressed, the way he lived, the way he got over on "The Man." I wanted furs, fedoras, flared trousers, long maxi coats and a Cadillac with a Rolls Royce style radiator cap and enlarged grill.

It never dawned on me that Superfly was a made-up story glorifying a lifestyle leading to prison or death.

Birds of a feather flock together, and I acquired more drug using pals older than me. Jackie Jack was one. Every sentence coming out of his mouth had "Jack" at the end instead of a period. If he saw a good-looking woman with a glorious Afro, he'd say, "She got a spottie ottie dopalicious funkfro, Jack." He'd respond to the sight of a fine-looking chick by saying, "She's some foxy lady, Jack." If he couldn't say "Jack," he wouldn't have been able to talk in complete sentences.

My older drug buddy introduced me to Tony Boy and Big D, who were total opposites. We've all known men of few words, but Tony Boy had the fewest of all. Big D's real name was Denvil, and he was a motor mouth always wanting to voice his opinion on everything. He told Tony Boy, "Your problem, my man, happened when you was born. Yo' momma tol' you, 'Son, you been given just so many words and when you use 'em up, you die.'" All Tony Boy had to say in response was, "Ah guess." Whenever any of us got tired of listening to Big D, we'd tell him, "Hey, zip your soup cooler, Jack."

Jackie Jack came from a home far different than mine. His parents were running the streets and seldom around, allowing us to do drugs at Jackie's place. He lived in a single story three-bedroom residence called a "basement home" because half of it was below ground level. Five people squeezed into its seven hundred square feet, less than half the space in my family's home. There was no back door, and a side entrance was the only way in or out.

My friends and I snorted mixed jive in a windowless room with concrete walls and ceiling that Jackie Jack shared with his older brother, Errol. A previous occupant of the house had applied furry strips of half-inch-thick insulation to the walls which absorbed moisture and made the room cold and damp. It didn't bother us. We lay on the floor, numb to the core.

Any time Jackie Jack's dark, miserable room wasn't free, we'd use my family's basement. If all else failed, we'd go to dope houses without any thought of what might go wrong. We knew where to go because heroin was easily obtained on Pontiac's south side. It was as if a smart bomb loaded with dope had been launched by an evil genius bent on eliminating African Americans. Pontiac was a great place for people with bad habits and so much dope was floating around, the corrupt cops became puppets of a drug lord and the honest ones were overwhelmed.

Our drug use reached another level when Big D learned about injecting heroin into his veins from his cousins. The next time he saw me he was singing the Temptations' tune "Cloud Nine."

"I took the climb to cloud nine. I'm doin' fine on cloud nine." He claimed it was a much better high than snorting, saying, "Man, it sent me past cloud nine to cloud eighteen!" Reed Carson, a married dude way older than me, introduced his younger brother, Jimmy, and me to mainlining. Jimmy was a high school quarterback who could throw a football the length of the field, but I was only twelve years old. The narcotic's voice reached out to my inner self and I let it take me by the hand.

We used the basement in my family's home to shoot up and nod out, and became careless about leaving used needles behind the freezer. You couldn't put anything past my mother, and it was inevitable she'd spot them and I'd be busted.

One morning, Momma woke me from a sound sleep and placed a dirty, blood stained hypodermic on my nightstand. She asked, "What do you call this?" and then caught a bus for work. Right was right and wrong was wrong, and I had done wrong and been caught. She let me agonize all day about how I would be punished.

Momma came home that evening after a long day of cleaning someone else's home. Neither of my parents would physically punish me once I had grown taller than them. Rather than wear my butt out with switches, my mother chose to have a serious talk with me. She began by saying, "Your trouble is you got too much time on your hands. You need to get a job."

"Who gonna hire a twelve-year-old?" I replied. "You can get a paper route."

"A paper route? Momma, I don't want no paper route! I make more'n a week than the paper boy make in a year."

I'll never forget the horribly sad look on her face when I said that. We had been best friends, but her baby boy was turning into a thug before her eyes. She was at a loss of what to do. I had become uncontrollable. I thought I knew everything, but really knew very little.

In April, 1972, when I was fourteen, Reed Carson, and his wife, Vernell, invited me to ride with them to Simms department store on Huron Street. When I got in the backseat, I noticed one of their kids had left a toy gun. I thought it would be fun to pretend I was kidnapping Reed and Vernell. Placing the barrel of the toy pistol against the back of Reed's head, I growled, "Do what I say and you'll live! Keep drivin'til I tell ya to stop." Reed went along with the game, not knowing we were being watched.

When Reed pulled up at the store, we were swarmed by twelve police officers. Some wore riot gear and carried shotguns. I heard an officer's voice over a bull horn. "Drop the gun, keep your hands in plain sight and slowly get out of the car."

I thought, *What am I gonna do? I got a nickel bag in my pocket.* I gulped as I held my hands up and slowly left Reed's vehicle.

A policeman was chuckling when he saw the pistol was a toy and realized I had been playing a stupid kid's game, but his expression changed when another officer found my bag of marijuana. I was arrested and my parents had to come for me. A court date was set and Mom and Dad were there when a judge sentenced me to six months probation and a weekend at the Oakland County Children's Village.

My mother and father had to drop me off at the Children's Village, and we drove there in my dad's 1959 Plymouth four door. It was arroyo blue with white trim and had a pushbutton automatic transmission. Dad didn't have much to say, but my mother was sobbing because her baby boy was going to a jail. She said repeatedly, "I knew this was gonna happen. I knew it, I knew it, I knew it."

As I stepped out of the car, I acted like a tough guy and said, "I can handle this.

No big deal."

My mother was weeping and my dad angrily shook a finger at me. He said, "No Thomas ever went to jail before! You think you're tough, but you're a fool. You got off easy this time, and it better be the end of it."

After entering the youth facility, I was led to a room with a set of bunk beds and a metal toilet bowl. Sinks and showers were in a room down the hall. My roommate was a kid with much darker skin and older than me, but much shorter and very skinny. He was laying on the bottom bunk and asked, "Who're you?"

"I'm Pinklon."

He made a derisive "Hummmph" sound and said, "Yo' momma musta been high ta give ya a dumb name like that!" He aggressively pointed to the upper bunk and said, "Ya'll sleep up theah." My roommate had mean eyes and since I was only going to be there for the weekend, I decided not to start anything.

I asked him, "What's your name?"

"Floyd."

"How long ya been here?"

"Too long," Floyd replied in a surly tone. He smirked and added, "Word is you only gonna be heah this weekend."

"Uh huh."

"Then there's no point in gettin' to know each other. Just stay outta my way. I'm colder'n concrete steps in the winter." Floyd got up from his bunk and headed for the day room to watch TV.

When meals were served, we had to line up and march single file to a cafeteria. We were expected to eat within ten minutes and if we weren't able to finish, that was just too bad. The food was horrible. What they called barbeque was a mustard and vinegar abomination. It couldn't compare to my mom and dad's cooking and I wasn't served nearly as much as I was used to.

I was so big for my age nobody tried to beat me up. No one talked to me except Floyd, when he felt like saying something nasty or ordering me around. He had probably been bullied and took full advantage of his chance to lord it over a bigger guy. It was a miserable two days, and the worst part was my loss of freedom. I was told when to get up, when to take a shower, when to eat and when to go to bed. I learned a lesson, but not the right one. Instead of vowing "I'll never do anything to get put back in a place like this," I promised myself "I'll never get caught again."

I was my worst enemy, my toughest opponent and that's just no joke, it's no lie. ... I was my own toughest opponent, a dummy and I made some crazy decisions."

BOB KAISER:
LITTLE BIG MAN

After my parents, the greatest blessing God granted me as a child was placing Bob Kaiser in my life. Only five foot two, he was the "The Biggest Little Man the World Has Ever Known." A light skinned black, he was an amazingly gifted athlete who excelled at wrestling, boxing and track and could have done very well at basketball if he weren't so short. He was a humble, upbeat guy who often said, "There's no need in cryin', ya gotta get busy tryin'. When you're short like me, ya gotta figure out ways to equalize the playin' field."

Bob graduated from Pontiac Central High School in 1959 and joined the Army the following year. He was placed in charge of a recreational facility and also did some wrestling and boxing. He performed well enough as a wrestler to be invited to try out for the 1964 Olympics. Discharged from the service in 1963, he returned to his hometown, not expecting to be around for more than a couple of months. Tryouts for the U.S. Olympic wrestling team were on the horizon and he had been offered a college wrestling scholarship.

His plans took an unforeseen turn when he injured both shoulders during a national wrestling tournament. He returned to Pontiac and went to work in a GM plant. Bob's passion for being involved in sports never left him, and he noticed how little there was to do after school for tens of thousands of kids in town. The pint sized athlete decided to remedy the situation.

He had earned the trust of many friends while growing up. One was Hubert Price, the custodian at Jefferson Junior High and Whittier Elementary School. The two schools were located next to each other and connected by a long hallway housing a cafeteria. Bob's friend allowed him access to the gymnasium and athletic field so he could conduct after school programs teaching fundamentals of various sports. His efforts were well received, and other men in the black community rallied to the cause and pitched in as volunteers. After twelve years of diligent volunteer labor, Pontiac's Mayor Walter Moore happened to stop by one summer afternoon. The mayor was always on the lookout for positive things to align with and noticed the large number of happy faced children Bob and his fellow volunteers were supervising. Mayor Moore asked, "How many kids are here?"

Bob replied, "Hundreds, give or take one or two."

"Who runs this program?"

The little man with a contagious smile replied, "Me and some other volunteers." The mayor shook his head and said, "Not anymore."

"Whadya mean?"

"It's our program now, but we're gonna pay you to run it." That was all it took for Bob Kaiser to be hired by the city of Pontiac. He continued working at the auto plant and later held down a third job, working for the school district as track coach at Jefferson Junior High. His schedule seemed nonstop, but he was a man of boundless energy who touched many lives.

I started participating in Bob Kaiser's programs when I was nine. The first things I learned from him were how to do sit ups and pushups properly. I was five eleven then, but hadn't begun to seriously pursue sports. I became more involved when I was eleven and being introduced to drugs by Slim, the track athlete.

I was hooked on heroin at twelve and couldn't hide it from Bob. He handled the situation in a compassionate way. He didn't go to my parents, but was able to have me enrolled in a methadone program. Bob encouraged me to devote more time to sports, especially football, basketball and track, because he knew the more active I was, the less chance of me getting high. He warned, "A moth is drawn to a flame and gets burned up on arrival. That poison will ruin your strength, speed and reflexes."

Under Bob's guidance, I developed as a track athlete. My events were the hundred-yard dash, the two twenty and running a leg of the four forty relay. Based on my coach's glowing recommendation, I was chosen to be part of Pontiac's AAU track squad. Bob said, "Pink runs like a thief with get away from the cops speed."

One of the athletes I competed against was Harlan Huckleby of the Detroit Striders, who had gotten into track to build up his lungs and endurance after suffering childhood asthma. Harlan always beat me, but never by more than a tenth of a second. He went on to play football and run track for the University of Michigan, appear in three Rose Bowls and win acclaim as a kick returner during six seasons with the Green Bay Packers. He's an example of what a young athlete can accomplish if they stay in school and enter pro sports through the front door. In looking back, I wish I had followed his path.

During this time, Ron Baker was the big boss of drug dealing in Pontiac and ruled his illegal empire with an iron hand. So seldom seen that few people could recognize him, everyone in his organization feared him because he would eliminate a person with no more thought than drinking a glass of water.

Ron grew up with Bob Kaiser and though different in so many ways, there was mutual respect between the two and they shared a passion for sports. The drug king's favorite was basketball, and he bankrolled a minor league pro team called the Pontiac Chaparrals. Legendary NBA star George "Iceman" Gervin played for the Chaparrals during the early 1970s, and Ron Baker was paying the Iceman five hundred a month while he was tearing up the Eastern Basketball Association.

Gervin was spotted by John "Red" Kerr, a scout for the Virginia Squires ABA team. On Kerr's recommendation, the Squires paid Ron Baker a hundred grand for the rights to Gervin. The big return on his investment convinced Baker there were more George Gervin's among the many basketball players who had dropped out of school or couldn't get along with their high school coaches. He worked with Bob Kaiser to create the Pontiac Junior Chaparrals, a team made up of fourteen to eighteen-year-old males.

The city of Pontiac was a basketball hotbed, and the local high school was renowned for its teams. Every year, the Pontiac Central High Chiefs were among the top-rated squads in the state and if they didn't win the state tournament, it was considered a disappointing season. There was a wealth of homegrown talent, but it was a turbulent time the Temptations sang about in their hit Ball of Confusion. "Evolution, revolution, gun control, sound of soul, shooting rockets to the moon, kids growing up too soon." So many of the city's basketball players had become sidetracked because of drugs, alcohol and dropping out of school that the Junior Chaparrals had as good and in many cases, better players than Pontiac Central High School.

Bob Kaiser wanted the Junior Chaparrals to be about much more than money. To join the team, we had to pay a price by convincing him we were trying to straighten out our lives. He knew we weren't perfect and probably weren't going to come all the way back, but we had to at least be trying. He expected us to meet certain standards, and this was a key ingredient in our becoming an outstanding team. Bob knew how important little things were and left no stone unturned in making practices enjoyable as well as productive. He went over details that led to success, such as the proper way of putting on our socks to prevent blisters. He also played jazz music while we practiced because of the relaxing, rhythmic atmosphere it created. From my positive association of jazz with the fun of playing basketball, I've had a lifelong appreciation of that form of music.

I was fourteen years old, six foot three and a hundred eighty pounds when the Junior Chaparrals were formed, and won a starting position. I was listed as a center, but could play any position Bob Kaiser wanted. I was big and strong enough to muscle toward the hoop, could lead the fast break, handle the ball, rebound and was deadly accurate in the paint.

The Junior Chaparrals became locally famous and all home games were standing room only sellouts. We were a team representing south Pontiac's underground economy, and our boisterous fans included dope dealers, numbers runners, pimps and other hustlers. Like Pontiac Central High, our games attracted big money bets and extensive coverage in the local papers, complete with photo spreads.

We weren't allowed to schedule high school teams and it was very difficult to find local AAU squads who could compete with us. Thanks to Ron Baker, we had money to travel in chartered buses all over the country and even Montreal to take on top flight competition. Every spring during Easter break, Bob took us to black colleges, like Tennessee State, Central State, Johnson C. Smith and the Laurinburg Institute in North Carolina, so we could play their varsity teams. Many of us were offered scholarships on the spot. I received offers, and the college coaches were surprised to learn I was only fourteen. They had no idea going to school was the last thing on my mind.

*"I made a lot of bad decisions going through junior high,
getting kicked out of high school and doing crazy stuff,
being on the run after trying to be a gangster.
It took its toll and only for the grace
that I'm here today to talk about it."*

SCHOOL DAYS?
NO WAY!

As exceptional as I was on the basketball court, I was a complete dud in the classroom. I was capable of doing the work and could read very well, but just didn't want to. I played hooky as often as I could and the few times I was in class, oozed indifference by slumping in my seat with half lidded eyes and often yawning. Very few teachers could deal with me because I didn't want to be in school, period. Talking to me was like talking to a tree and I saw no joy in becoming an educated person. I thought, *The future don't exist and the past already happened, so only today counts. Why worry about stuff in books? I don't need no school. I was born smart.*

Instead of improving my mind, developing God-given talents and maturing, I was counterpunching against reality. By clouding my brain with drugs, I was allowing my thinking process to waste away from inactivity.

Few of my teachers could motivate me the way Bob Kaiser did, and too many seemed to be going through the motions and marking time until retirement. This doesn't excuse my behavior. I was rebellious, very foolish and my own worst enemy. If stupidity were music, I would have been a band.

I was looking to the wrong men as role models. My father and Bob Kaiser were great ones, but they weren't as cool as underlings of local drug king Ron Baker and other hustlers I saw on a daily basis. Those of the "cool world" wore flashier clothes, drove new cars and made more than people doing honest work. I didn't grow up in a ghetto, but yearned for a ghetto way of life; complete with Cadillacs, "pimplicious threads," gaudy jewelry and the power of a pistol in my hand. School wouldn't teach me the ways of the street, where the real fun and easy living was. I often wonder where I got such insane ideas from. I certainly didn't inherit them or learn them at home because my parents were God fearing, honest, hardworking people, striving for class and dignity.

When I was fourteen, I could whip a grown man. By the time I was fifteen, I was six three, one hundred ninety pounds and could run the hundred in 10.5 seconds. I was hanging with guys in their twenties engaged in criminal activities who all carried guns. Most had cars and cash. I was bigger and stronger than them and had a reputation as a street fighter. They nodded their approval when I boasted, "I'm a thrill seeker and rider of the storm who keeps on truckin', don't matter the weather's wet or warm." They looked upon me as their enforcer, and this meant I had to have my own weapon.

It was easier to buy bullets and guns than food in south Pontiac. If a person were to go into a small neighborhood store and ask for lunch meat or a loaf of rye, they'd be told, "Don't have any today." But ask for bullets, and the response would be, "Just a minute," and whoever was behind the counter would go in the back and come out with ammunition. After being paid, they would ask, "Sure you don't need more'n that?" There were few legal guns in my neighborhood, but it seemed like everybody except my mom and dad had at least one pistol. Age meant nothing. If you had the connection, you got the protection. This was true even for fifteen-year-old goofs like me.

Another distraction I faced was forced busing. It started when I was in the eighth grade and led to many kids going to seven different schools in twelve years and seeing angry adults throwing rocks at school buses. Back then, elementary school went from kindergarten to sixth grade. Seventh, eighth and ninth were junior high. I attended Jefferson Junior High for seventh grade, Washington Junior High on the west side for eighth grade and was bused to Lincoln Junior High in the northeast section of Pontiac for ninth grade.

I had little interest in my classes or even the sports offered at Jefferson Junior High. I took my delight in wickedness and went there strictly to make money selling marijuana to the other kids. I towered over all the other guys, even the ninth graders, and dressed far more stylishly. The only time I wore basketball shoes was when I was on the court.

Dr. Reginald Nell, the school's principal, caught me selling weed in the hallway one day. I had just transacted two joints for a buck and slipped the money into my pocket when he showed up from out of nowhere. A man with very dark skin, Dr. Nell was as tall as me, but much heavier. He snatched the bag of marijuana from my hands, grabbed me by the back of my shirt collar and walked me to his office.

The pot-bellied principal squeezed his bulk into a high backed swivel chair and sat with the package of pot in front of him. He pointed to a wooden chair in front of his desk and said, "Sit." I sat down, not knowing what to expect. Would he scream and holler? Would he call the cops? Would he notify my parents?

Speaking in a calm voice, he asked, "What do you call yourself doing?"

"Just tryin' to make some money… sir." I figured it wouldn't hurt to be polite.

He said, "We've got the City Championship Track Meet coming up. Why don't you get it together? You could win."

"Nah, ain't my circus and ain't my monkey," I replied. I knew it would mean putting in a lot of work to get ready and I would have to lay off the drugs while I trained.

He peered at me over the top of his glasses, held up the confiscated bag of weed and asked, "What if we forget about this and I don't tell your parents or the police?"

I could see where things were headed. I had a choice of running for Jefferson Junior High or having parents and police involved. I gave out a loud sigh of resignation and said, "Okay, I'll run in the track meet."

"Fine, I'll tell the coach you'll be at practice this afternoon."

My reply was, "Cool, man." Knowing he had me, Dr. Nell smiled like a Cheshire cat.

Over the next three weeks, I stayed away from dope, worked out every day and got in great shape. Jefferson won the city meet and I set records in the two-twenty and the four-forty relay. Once the track meet was over, I went back to dealing weed and using drugs.

Not long after that, I heard an announcement over the school P.A. system. "Pinklon Thomas, report to the principal's office." I thought, *They gonna pat me on the back and tell me good things 'bout myself.* When I arrived at Dr. Nell's office, the door was open wide enough for me to see my mother and father sitting there. Despair was written all over their faces. I didn't walk in and stood outside listening.

I heard the principal say. "I caught Pinklon selling marijuana, so I'm going to suspend him for the rest of the year." There were only two and a half months before school was out for the summer. Dr. Nell had lied and double crossed me just to satisfy his ego.

The next year, I was bused to Washington Junior High on the west side for eighth grade and assigned to Al "Bulldog" Thomas' homeroom. He was also the school's disciplinary teacher and held detention during school hours. Al had been a professional wrestler and moonlighted as a pro wrestling referee, often officiating matches featuring legends such as the Sheik and Bobo Brazil, who I enjoyed watching on TV.

I spent more time in Al Thomas' disciplinary classes than in my regular classes. He believed in physical activity as a way of keeping kids out of trouble. Rather than force me to do things that bored me and made me feel trapped, he taught me the proper way to skip rope and lift weights. He asked, "Do you like boxing?"

When I said I did, he replied, "This Saturday, I'm gonna take you somewhere I know you'll enjoy."

Saturday arrived, and Bulldog Thomas drove me to the gym in the King Solomon Baptist Church on Detroit's 14th Street. I hit the bags, skipped some rope and my teacher was very encouraging. Unfortunately, I wasn't focused enough to train on a daily basis. I made the mistake of thinking I knew how to fight, based on that one trip to the gym. The King Solomon church was a long way from my home, and I had no way of getting there. It was more convenient doing what I was doing and I foolishly thought my athletic skills were all in place.

Later that year, an assembly was held so students could perform for the entire school. One of them was a girl who played the piano. One look at her and I thought, *Oooh, looky there! Whatta knockout!* After her performance ended, the principal asked, "Does anyone have anything to say?"

Sitting with some friends, I piped up and said, "Could you have that girl with the outta sight Afro and big earrings came over to see me? I'd like to talk to her." My friends broke out in laughter. The principal said, "Be quiet, Mr. Thomas. Not one part of your existence is enjoyable for anyone. I'm beginning to envy those who never had to meet you."

I didn't meet the girl that day, but later found out her name was Kathy Jones. She began hanging out with me. We shared an interest in music, but she was a year older, much more motivated, made good grades and was determined to get somewhere. The tall, talented young woman with the Afro fell for me and I really admired her.

In her infatuation, she had no idea where money for my wardrobe and good times came from. She didn't press me to find out the truth, and I revealed nothing about my criminal enterprises. I knew if I did, she probably wouldn't have had a thing to do with me. I was not acting honorably by hiding my true self from a woman who was becoming romantically connected to me. The streets had taught me an evil lesson: "Secrets must be kept in order to survive."

LIVING AND NEARLY DYING BY THE GUN

I was fifteen and finally off probation when I became a womanizer. I was more interested in Kathy Jones but in my selfish, wrongheaded state, I looked at the other girls as ones to have fun with. We had unprotected sex and five became pregnant at roughly the same time. Two were expecting twins. I couldn't imagine having to support seven children and told each one, "Go get an abortion. I'm only fifteen. Can't pay for no babies!"

Three got abortions, including the two carrying twins. Of the two who wouldn't go along with my cold-hearted suggestion, one was Althea, a young woman a year older than me. After telling her I couldn't do anything for her, she went to see my father, who had known her as a little girl growing up.

Dad laid down the law to me, saying, "Junior, be a man and do the right thing.

Marry the girl."

I replied, "Got no job and no money."

His response was, "Well then, keep your butt in school and graduate. In the meantime, I can help you find part time work. You can't be thinkin' only of yourself, not with a child to support. Don't you have a conscience?"

I felt like saying, "My conscience don't bother me and I don't bother it," but chose not to respond and sat there smirking. The disgusted look on my dad's face spoke volumes about how deeply I disappointed him. From the way I was behaving, there was little hope of my becoming a man of honor. Real men don't tell their conscience, "I'll call ya when I need ya." Lacking long term thinking and living moment to moment, I closed my mind to my father's wisdom. This was the way of a child, not a mature person. Showing no concern for Althea and our unborn child, I did nothing for her.

Mom and Dad came through and helped her a great deal. Althea gave birth to a baby girl in November, 1973 and named the child PaQuana. My parents tried to make up for my being an absent father by treating PaQuana as doting grandparents would.

Shirking all responsibility, I stopped going to school, acquired several handguns and spent my time, playing for the Junior Chaparrals and robbing restaurants. I foolishly believed if I got caught, all the authorities would do was send me back to the Oakland County Children's Village. Having been there for a weekend, I thought I knew the ropes and felt I could handle it. The possibility of being charged as an adult never crossed my mind. I thought, *I can run fast and my hands are quick. If I'm in and out of the place in less than two minutes, I'll be cool. I'll do it so fast, cops won't be able to collar me.* That was the thinking of a fool, not a rational person.

It wasn't just being hooked on drugs. I had become addicted to the gangster lifestyle. It offered intoxicating excitement, a chance to match wits, the adrenaline rush of facing danger and the feeling of power when holding a loaded handgun. I didn't bother to conceal my face because I wanted people to see my menacing features. It thrilled me to scare people. I was too dumb to realize the refreshing, but enmeshing, kicks I found in crime were part of a race to death.

Gangsters end up alone and miserable because there's no honor or bonds of brotherhood among such cold-hearted souls. If one tells another, "I promise," they usually mean "Maybe I will and maybe I won't," "We'll see." or at best "I'll try." When one rips off another, they never apologize, but say, "Be's that way sometimes." They'll do in any of their friends if it means getting what they want. "The Man" makes the rules, but gangsters think they can bend 'em and break 'em. They are dead wrong because there's no such thing as a perfect crime. One way or another, every gangster gets it in the end, and street rats are mourned only by their fleas.

My mom and dad never knew exactly what I was up to, but were sure I was involved in dangerous things. They felt powerless to stop me, and it wore away at them. My sister Bernice once told me, "When you're not home, Momma jumps whenever she hears a siren. She worries it might be for you." My parents were praying for me and some of their prayers were answered, otherwise I would have ended up in prison or dead.

I put my life and the lives of innocent people in jeopardy for peanuts. By committing armed robberies, I risked being arrested, prosecuted and sentenced to a "football number," pulling a long stretch in a state prison.

Robbing local businesses was insanity. Once I robbed one, I could never go there again. This made the small world of my neighborhood even more cramped.

Bob Kaiser was driving me home from basketball practice one night and said, "Pink, let's get somethin' to eat."

"Okay, Bob."

He drove to a shopping center right behind both our houses. My coach pulled up to a Chinese restaurant. I said, "We can't go in there."

"Why?"

"'Cuz I robbed 'em."

Bob said, "Okay, we'll go down to the McDonald's"

"Can't go there either."

"Why?"

"I robbed them too."

"How many restaurants have you robbed in our neighborhood?"

"All of 'em." We had to go to another part of the city for something to eat.

In addition to armed robbery, I was continuing to use drugs purchased at dope dens riddling the neighborhood. I would walk up to the door, knock and was never sure of what would happen next. If the person opening the door recognized me, I was allowed to enter. Once inside, I was watched closely by people uncomfortable to be around. I would hand over my money, hope I wasn't ripped off and leave immediately after receiving the merchandise. It always made me uneasy to be in those places, but I felt I had no choice because my system needed the dope.

Some drug houses wouldn't open the door. I would put money in a slot and a minute or so later, drugs would come out from the same opening. I often worried about dropping money in, but not receiving any dope. This would have made me feel very uncool.

There was also the danger that cops would kick down the doors and raid the drug den while I was there. If I got caught up in a raid, I'd be taken to jail along with everyone else in the place. How would I explain that to my parents?

I was never caught in a raid, but there were times dope houses were raided immediately after I left them. This posed a danger for me because I could have been accused of ratting out the place. Snitches get stitches or end up in ditches with bullets in their heads. A child playing at being a man, I had put myself into a deadly serious world where violent people played for keeps. If I had been given an IQ test at that point in my life, I would have come out with a minus score.

I needed money to support my drug habit, which had grown to a hundred bucks a day. Since there were no more neighborhood restaurants to rob, I had to come up with an idea, and my craving for heroin affected my thinking. I decided to take down a stash house operated by Clyde and his enforcer Shotgun Steve. This was moronic. Steve was a vicious man with skin the color of dark chocolate; tough as nails, but blind as Mr. Magoo. He used a sawed-off pump action shotgun to have a better chance of hitting something.

I targeted Clyde's place because he was one of the dealers who allowed customers inside. I had bought dope there numerous times, and they jokingly called me "Shorty" because I was so tall. Clyde, a dealer with jet black skin, appeared flush with cash. He had a brand-new yellow Plymouth Barracuda with a 440 Magnum engine that he kept so clean you could eat off the valve covers. I foolishly thought he wouldn't get too upset over losing a few hundred bucks worth of drugs.

It was in the winter, and the idea of pulling the robbery came to me on the spur of the moment during a heavy snowfall. I saw some dudes with ski masks covering their heads and a light bulb went on in my little used brain. I thought, *I'll put on a ski mask and no one'll know it's me.* It was a perfect plan, or so I thought.

Low visibility from the hard snowfall made it difficult to navigate sidewalks. Few cars or pedestrians were around as I made my way to the dope den. I knocked on Clyde's door. Shotgun Steve answered, and wasn't holding his weapon. I thought, *This is gonna be easy.*

Steve gazed at me through thick lenses resembling cat's eye marbles and said, "Man in charge'll be back in a few minutes. It's murder out there with all the snow, but he's almost finished diggin' out his car. Well, get in here! Ain't gonna heat the whole neighborhood."

Knowing I had very little time, I frantically scanned the front room, wondering where money or drugs might be kept. Suddenly, I spotted a partially opened drawer containing packets of heroin. The vision impaired drug enforcer went to the window to see if his boss might be coming, and I made my move. In a flash, I pulled out my .357 magnum and clobbered him over the head. He dropped like a sack of wet sand.

Yanking open the drawer, I grabbed as many packets I could cram into my pockets. I opened three more drawers before finding a stack of bills in a small cardboard box without a lid. I bolted from the house before the enforcer woke up or Clyde came in. Lucky to keep my footing as I ran through the snow, I made it back to my home, went to the basement and sorted out my plunder. There was two hundred in cash and thirty hits of heroin. I felt an adrenaline rush after pulling off the perfect crime and thought, "I can see myself doin' this again."

Next day, the storm was over, the sun was out, but it was still cold. Kathy and I were walking along my street. It was three o'clock and she had just gotten out of school. I was distracted from our conversation when I saw Clyde's yellow Barracuda go by. I thought, *They ain't rollin' up on me. It's broad daylight and how would Clyde know I ripped 'im off. Steve couldn't tell it was me.* I put all thoughts of Clyde and Shotgun Steve out of my mind.

That night, I was on my way to Jackie Jack's house, planning to meet up with him and Big D and share some heroin with them. Halfway there, Clyde pulled up in his Barracuda. He double parked, jumped out of his car with a Colt .45 automatic in hand and came toward me, shouting, *"Where's my drugs, pink? Where's my drugs?"*

I thought, *How he know it was me?* I was really idiotic back then. I shrugged with palms up and said, "Don't know what you talkin' 'bout."

"Don't gimme that jive. *Where's my drugs?*"

I had left my gun in its usual hiding place, under the mattress of my bed. Clyde was no more than four feet from me and in my mentally unbalanced state I was thinking, "If he come just a coupla feet closer, I can nail him." I was crazy enough to take on a gunman with my fists.

Our encounter came to an abrupt end when irate motorists began honking at Clyde for blocking the street. He hopped back in his car and pulled away with tires squealing. I deserved to die, but God must have loved and protected me even though I was acting so insane.

The next night, I was out walking with Jackie Jack and Big D. Once again, I was unarmed because my piece was still under the mattress. I had foolishly led my partners down the same street as Clyde's drug house. I saw his yellow Barracuda turn the corner and thought, "Here we go again!" They rolled by and then stopped thirty yards from us. I shouted, *"Every man for himself and God for us all!"* as I took off running. There was still snow on the ground and I gulped in wintry night air as I ran for my life. The frantic pace of my feet made slapping sounds on the damp pavement. Metal trash barrels and mounds of snow were all along the street. Clyde and Shotgun Steve fired four times each and I heard bullets penetrate garbage cans. I continued in an all-out sprint, hoping to make it to Club Plush, a neighborhood nightspot.

There was panic in my stride, wild unreasoning panic. I had underestimated how it would feel if someone were shooting at me. Arriving at the club in one piece, I found the place closed. I blurted out, "They closed! What I'm gonna do now?" Singlemindedly focused on staying alive, I ran another two miles through back streets and had to vault a chain link fence before reaching home. Once again, God kept me in His hand and in His infinite mercy, didn't close His fist too tight.

The following night was basketball practice and Bob Kaiser drove me home. When I got out of his car, I glanced down my street and saw the dreaded yellow Barracuda coming toward me from the other direction. This time, I had a .357 Magnum in my gym bag. Clyde and Shotgun Steve skidded to a stop and bolted out of the yellow muscle car with guns blazing before I could pull my pistol from my bag. I dove for the ground behind a tree wide enough to conceal me and crouched out of sight. Their aim hadn't improved and I wasn't hit, but my luck couldn't hold out forever.

Gunplay lasted less than a minute before my attackers made a rubber burning exit. I thought, *They gonna keep tryin'. What I'm gonna do?* Still crouched behind the tree, I felt a hand on my shoulder. I spun around with the magnum in my hand, ready to fire. It was Bob. Only a split second of recognition kept me from shooting a man who was a second father to me. He said, "Put that away and get in the car. We gotta go somewhere and talk."

He drove to a snack shop in another part of the city where I hadn't robbed any restaurants. I ordered a catfish sandwich and ate while he talked. Somehow it didn't taste as good as it usually did. I had lost my appetite and thought, "What if I won't be able to eat as long as those two are gunnin' for me?"

My coach asked, "Why they tryin' to kill you?"

I came correct. I couldn't hide what I'd done from him because he was determined to get to the bottom of it. I felt I could trust him because he had kept my being in a methadone program secret. I told him all about robbing Clyde's drug den. Bob said, "Who do you think you stole from?"

"Clyde," I replied.

"Wrong. You stole from Ron Baker, the man who put up the money for our basketball team. He's Mr. Big for drugs in this city. Ron prolly told Clyde, 'Bring me the drugs or bring me his head.' There's a contract out on you."

Bob shook his head for a moment before saying, "Pink, I had a dream three nights ago. You were bein' introduced before one of our games. When you walked out on the court, a guy in the stands stood up. He had a gun and shot you. You died in my arms, and I woke up cryin'."

He took a sip of his Pepsi and then asked, "Whatta you think's gonna happen at our next game? They may try to kill you then and there and might hit innocent bystanders. Until this mess is solved, you can't play no more."

"I'm gonna play," I blurted out. "I ain't afraid."

"It's not just you. You'll be puttin' others in danger."

"What ya gonna do, Bob? You're not gonna keep me from playin', are ya? It's the only thing keeps me from gettin' high."

He was silent for a moment before replying, "I'm gonna try somethin'. I'm takin' ya to see Ron Baker. When you're standin' in front of him, look like you're sorry for what ya did, but don't say a word. I'll do all the talkin'."

Bob Kaiser and the drug king had grown up together and he was close enough to the man that he could intercede and plead for me. While Bob drove to Baker's headquarters, I thought, *What if the big man won't gimme a break? I'll hafta rob somebody else to pay him.*

Ron Baker's place wasn't what I expected. It was a three-story residence with a wooden front porch as wide as the house itself. My coach knocked on the front door and one of Baker's bodyguards who knew Bob opened it. He said, "How's it goin' Bobby? How's the team look?"

"Great, gonna win our next game easy. Boss in?"

"Third floor, you know the way."

Three more bodyguards were sitting in the front room. A television was on, but all eyes were watching Bob and me. I wondered, "Do they know there's a contract on me?" Fear caused a drop of sweat to roll all the way down my back to my waist. My throat was closing up as I followed Bob up the stairs to the big man's third floor office. I expected to be met by a menacing seven-foot giant with rippling muscles.

I was surprised to find Ron Baker was short, skinny and bald, but his eyes were like hot coals and I could feel them burn into me. I thought, *It's all up to him. Is he gonna kill me on the spot?*

This was no social call, and Ron didn't ask us to take a seat. He sat at his desk while we stood. Bob spoke first. "My man, I want you to take that hit off this knucklehead." Bob nodded toward me. Ron stared at my basketball coach for a moment, then said, "Okay, Bob, 'cuz of you, I'll see what I can do to take it off him. But I'm tellin' ya now, if he do it again, he gotta go. And you know what that means, dontcha? You gotta go with him."

Bob turned toward me and said, "If ya do somethin' else, I'll shoot ya myself." I was no longer bothered by Clyde and Shotgun Steve. I never repaid Ron Baker for the cash or drugs, but kept playing for the Junior Chaparrals and the team continued to win, which fed the drug king's ego. He was as proud of his basketball teams as an owner of a Derby winner or Super Bowl champ. Maybe Ron wrote off what I stole as a gift for helping his team win so many games.

I still hadn't learned my lesson and continued riding the wings of devastation. I was hanging out at a pool room on Saginaw Street owned by a man named Gabby. One of the regulars was a dude known as Geronimo, an addict from Boston. Standing five foot nine, he had big shoulders, big thighs, twenty-inch biceps and a slim waist. His arms were shorter than normal but if he got close enough, his deadly, vice-like hands could crumble bones or squeeze a head until it popped. As a fifteen-year-old, I should never have been hanging around such a volatile combination of physical power and drug crazed behavior.

Geronimo came in while I was shooting a game of pool. From the way he staggered, I could tell he was high. He tried to pull a clear plastic bag of Quaaludes from his pocket, but fumbled and dropped it on the floor. I quickly reached for the pills, and he shouted, *"I dare you to pick 'em up!"*

I should have been scared, but wasn't, so I picked up the bag. Suddenly, I felt fierce pain in my head. The light skinned black muscle man had hit me with the thick back end of a pool cue. I felt all over my scalp and was relieved to find no blood on my hand. I looked at the owner of the pool room and said, "Gabby, I'm not doin' nothin' in here, but Geronimo gotta go outside with me."

Gabby replied, "Man, you don't wanna mess with him. The boy can do a hunnert pushups in nothin' flat."

I was so full of myself I replied, "Gabby, my man, I don't care what he done before. He hit me in the head with a pool stick, and he gotta pay."

I was acting like an idiot and wasn't thinking about the possibility of Geronimo being armed. I strutted out onto the sidewalk in front of Gabby's place. The addict twenty years older and thirty pounds heavier than me followed. Striking with the speed of a king cobra, I flipped him onto his back, then jumped on top and landed six quick punches to his face. As I introduced him to the pavement, a side of his head scraped against the concrete and the top of his ear was nearly taken off. The only sensible thing I did that night was head home right after the fight and not try to grab Geronimo's bag of 'ludes.

I could have suffered a serious head injury when Geronimo walloped me with the pool cue, and had placed myself in further danger by demanding he fight me on the sidewalk. I had been lucky, but luck doesn't last forever. I had positioned myself in a world where the meanest survived. It was only a matter of time until I was confronted by someone more vicious and powerful who could turn me into a disembodied nobody. A sane person would have been thinking of ways to return to school or get out of Pontiac, but I had no common sense at that point and was acting like an imbecile.

I teamed up with a cat named Doc for armed robberies. Five years older than me, he had a set of wheels. He would wait in the car while I went in and did the stickup. One time, I entered a business and saw a guy I knew. I didn't say a word, but glared at him and my menacing look sent the message, "I'll shoot you if you spill the beans." So, he acted like he didn't know me. I robbed the joint and made it to Doc's car before cops arrived.

One time, we did things differently. Doc and I drove to another part of Pontiac and entered a Chinese restaurant through the back entrance. The back door was wide open because the place had closed for the night and workers were busy cleaning up and hauling out trash. We opened the door to the manager's office and found a middle-aged Asian man sitting at a desk, going over the day's receipts. Doc pointed his handgun at him and snarled, "We want all the money."

With fear in his eyes, he peered at us over the top of his glasses and meekly said, "Money's in the safe." Doc said in a menacing tone, "Open it."

The restaurant owner wasn't the sort to kill anyone or let somebody die, so he obeyed my partner. When the door to the large floor safe was opened, I saw a snub nose .38, which I immediately snatched. We were lucky the Asian was too intimidated to go for his gun. He pleaded with us when we began to gag him and tie him up. "Please don't do that. I won't call the police." We saw the look of fear in his eyes and Doc felt a rush of power from frightening the man. We let him alone and left with the cash. The restaurant workers, so intent on finishing the cleaning and heading home, didn't notice us. As holdup men, we were careless and inept, but very, very lucky.

It was our biggest score: Two grand and a handgun. Doc put practically his entire share into his arm. His heroin habit had gotten out of control, and I began to worry he would become unreliable. I said to him, "Man, I think you're gonna hafta lighten up on the stuff. I don't want ya noddin' out while waitin' in the car."

He gave a harsh reply. "Don't tell me what to do. You tryin' ta out slick a can of oiI. I been usin' long before you been, and I can handle it."

There was no use talking to him. Doc had stopped being my partner and pal because he was already dead. All that was missing was the coffin.

I never saw him again. He tried to go it alone and went after a dope house belonging to three-hundred-pound Country Grimes. Doc stole cash and drugs, not knowing how well connected the dealer was. Within a week of his score, my former partner was shot dead at close range, execution style.

I was still hooked on being a gangster because there was big money to be made on the streets for hustlers willing to take risks and it made me feel important to be one of them. A tall, handsome cat named Warren Hodge was an All-State basketball player who had many scholarship offers, but turned them all down. He believed he could make more illegally than with a degree or even playing in the pros. When he got out of Pontiac Central High, he became a pimp known as "Jitterbug." Within a week of his graduation, he was driving a gold Lincoln Continental, smoking Kools and styling in oversized hats with feathers and purple suits. His meteoric rise made him a south Pontiac legend. I thought, *If he can do it, so can I.*

Jitterbug had been pimping a while when I turned sixteen. He hung out at the Big Six, an after-hours joint on Western and Bagley owned by my Uncle Charley and Aunt Liza. It offered dice games and other illegal gambling and would open after the Club Eighty-Eight bar across the street closed for the night. My uncle and auntie lived above their club. They once owned a Laundromat and did so well that they bought a building and turned the bottom part of it into the Big Six. They found it more profitable to conduct business while those leading normal lives were asleep.

As the star of the Junior Chaparrals, I was always in the papers and became caught up in how important I thought I had become. Late at night, when most sixteen-year-olds were resting up for their next day's classes, I decided to go to the Big Six, check out the action and maybe shoot some dice.

Approaching the gambling den, I saw Jitterbug standing at the entrance, a Colt .45 tucked in his waistband, "Mexican style." He was expounding to another cat on his theory of pimping. "The game's how you treat your womens, know what I'm sayin'? Woman gotta know when she out there, she makin' MY money. She be my bottom lady, she rank higher than all the other womens, but she still a woman workin' for ME, know what I'm sayin'? I gotta be out there every day keepin' my womens in line. Can't let 'em go shoppin', spendin' MY money on stupid junk. They gotta think 'That's Jitterbug's money,' know what I'm sayin'?"

Jitterbug noticed me soaking up his every word and said, "Hey, young blood!

Get your butt outta here and stay off the streets!"

He made it clear he didn't want me anywhere near him. I had foolishly believed pimping and other hustles were like sports, where older dudes helped young bloods break into the game. I thought, *He don't want me to be bigger'n better than him, or maybe he's thinkin' I'll try reachin' into his pocket.* I didn't want any trouble with Jitterbug, so I steered clear of the Big Six.

The combination of Jitterbug's warning and Doc's death greatly affected me. I began using even more drugs. I also began to think about getting out of Pontiac. I had come to realize my life was turning into a black hole, like the barrel of a gun, and if I stayed there, I would end up in prison or dead at a young age.

Jitterbug, the pimp with the Colt .45, eventually saw the handwriting on the wall and left the flesh peddling racket. It took some time, but he got his life together and became a substitute teacher. The whores who wasted their best years turning tricks and giving all the money to Jitterbug had fewer options. They were trapped in drug addiction and had to continue with prostitution to support their habits. One of them got busted and snitched her way out of trouble. She took the authorities to where Jitterbug buried the bones of a rival pimp he killed. The cops went to his school and walked the reformed pimp out in handcuffs. He was sentenced to life in prison and remains there to this day, dancing with the devil on a cold cell block. If anyone thinking of committing a criminal act could see what the horrendous consequences would be, very few would go through with it. Nobody gets away with breaking the law and one way or another, everyone pays. Just ask Jitterbug. He'd be the first to tell you, "Ain't no paradise for hustlers. They all get it in the end, know what I'm sayin'?"

I LITERALLY SHOOT MYSELF IN THE FOOT

I wanted to leave Pontiac, but still couldn't get the gangster life out of my system. One night while walking along Rapid Street, a Pontiac Bonneville four door pulled up. Dottie Conaway was behind the wheel and Willie Love was in the front passenger seat. They were on their way to meet up with friends living in a housing project and asked me to go along. I knew Willie. He was in his middle twenties, five eleven and two fifty. His last name was Love, but only brutality was in his heart. It was rumored he once said, "Ya can't kill me 'cuz I was born bullet proof." Willie had skill with a knife and could cut a dude so fast the victim wouldn't know he'd been sliced until it was too late to stop the bleeding. His street name was "Wicked Willie Slice 'N Dice."

Dottie was three years older than him, weighed over two hundred pounds and had unusually large hands for a woman. She had the disposition of an alligator, the nastiness of a rhinoceros and it was said when she snored, she exhaled smoke. Dottie used her Pontiac as a jitney cab and was also a "wheel lady" for robbers needing a getaway driver. She packed a wallop, toted a straight razor and once nearly beat a man to death with an extension cord. Dottie and Willie formed a lethal couple. They never tried to harm me, so I foolishly thought of them as friends. I had yet to learn there were no true friendships among hardened criminals.

Driving to the party, we spotted another of our fellow acquaintances named Andrew Gladney. We picked him up and he got in the backseat with me. I had never seen Andrew so excited. He blurted out, "Biggest roll I ever seen!"

"What you talkin' 'bout?" asked Willie.

Andrew said, "Man, you know that cat Bernie Muldrew?"

"Yeah, he run numbers. What 'bout 'im?".

"He had a roll this big." Andrew held his hands apart as if they were wrapped around a large grapefruit.

A smile creased Willie Love's face. He said, "Pink, ya got that .32 Smith and Wesson ya just bought on ya?"

"Naw, it's at home."

"We'll drop ya'll off at your place, then come back for ya. I wanna see it." They let me off in front of my house. Dad was out, Momma was over at my sister

Bernice's and I was alone. Bernice felt nothing but kindness toward me. She was a hard worker, who did well in school and held down part time jobs. After graduating from high school, she began a career in healthcare and was able to purchase a brand-new Ford LTD.

I took my Smith and Wesson from under my mattress and stood at the front window watching for Dottie's gray Pontiac. While I waited to be picked up and taken to the party, I fooled around with my new pistol, twirling it on my finger like a cowboy in a western. The gun suddenly went off and the recoil caused me to drop it. A bullet entered my right foot, near a toe. It felt like boiling water was pouring over my foot. I couldn't put weight on it and as I hopped to the telephone, I felt a balloon of intense heat inflating in my body. I dialed my sister's number and when my mother was on the line, said in a panicky voice, "Momma, I shot myself by accident! Come get me and take me to the hospital!"

Bernice and Momma were there within minutes, helped me into my sister's white LTD and took me to the emergency room. By the time we arrived, I was drenched in sweat and writhing in pain. I was given morphine and nodded out.

When I awoke, Momma was at my bedside. She said, "They asked me what happened and I told 'em it was an accident. You were playin' with a gun that didn't belong to you. I said you learned a lesson the hard way and I can't imagine you wantin' anything more to do with guns. The doctors had to take the bullet out. They said you were lucky it didn't bust into little pieces and tear up things inside your foot." With sad eyes, she asked, "You're not gonna have any more to do with guns, are you?"

"No Momma. Had my fill of 'em." This was a lie. From the look on her face I knew I had seen the last of my Smith and Wesson. Momma saw that the pistol was disposed of, but had no idea how many handguns I had. She didn't understand how important firearms were for surviving in the world I had chosen to become part of.

After four days in the hospital, I was released on crutches with an orthopedic pad on my heavily bandaged right foot. My first night home, I chilled out while Momma straightened the hair of one of her regular customers. The phone rang and when I answered it, Big D was on the line. He said, "Bernie Muldrew's dead. Found his body in the park. Somebody got all his money."

"Who did it?" I asked.

"Whoever iced him used a .32. You just got one a few days ago, didn't ya?"

"It wasn't me, Big D. Just got outta the hospital. Shot myself in the foot."

My drug buddy said he'd get the word out about my being in the hospital and then hung up. I had been told I would be laid up for a while, so I had to get used to staying around the house rather than running the streets.

Big D called the next day and said, "Dude, you and Willie Love got paper on yo' heads for killin' Muldrew."

I couldn't believe it. "A contract on me? Why? I was in the hospital."

"Mosta the money Muldrew had belonged to his boss. The boss found out you was talkin' 'bout the money with Willie. They also knows Willie wanted to see your gun."

"Who told 'em that?"

"Andrew Gladney."

I thought, *They musta made him talk.* My stomach was tied in knots and the stress of being accused made me stammer. "I... I... I been in the hospital four days! How could I be two places at once? They can't fit me into a frame, they just can't!"

"They say you might've killed him and then shot yo'self on purpose to get in the hospital and have an alibi. They also think you might not've pulled the trigger, but you coulda loaned Willie your piece and split the money with 'im."

"What do I do? "

"Don't go outta the house and stay away from windows."

I thought, *I can't believe this is happening!* I began to tremble uncontrollably and felt something grab my guts. I had never been so frightened before. When the contract had been put on me for robbing Clyde's dope house, I was able to run and wasn't forced to stay in with a bad foot. I thought, *If they try to kill me here in the house, they could kill Mom and Dad too!* I was so worried I couldn't sleep a wink that night, feeling as though I were trapped in a gray web woven by a thousand spiders.

Two more nights with precious little sleep followed before I got a call from Big D. He had good news. "Hit men took out a cat named Nubbie who was in on Muldrew's killing. Before he died, Nubbie confessed he and Willie Love killed Muldrew." I knew the guy Big D was talking about. He got his name because four fingers were missing from his right hand. Word on the street was the fingers were chopped off for stealing from someone he shouldn't have messed with. Big D once said, "If Nubbie tried to smack ya in the face with his right, he could only give ya half a slap."

A weight had been lifted from my shoulders. I asked Big D, "What 'bout Willie?"

"Nobody know where he at, and Dottie Conaway missin' too."

I began to worry again. I asked Big D, "What if Willie and Dottie come after ME?" He calmed my fears by saying, "They prolly a long way from here. Turns out Willie was on the run 'cuz he killed somebody 'bout a month ago. He needed money and decided to go after Muldrew. Nubbie also said Willie was first gonna take your Smith and Wesson from ya and woulda killed ya if he had to. He ran into Nubbie 'fore he got to you and decided it'd be better to cut him in than try takin' Muldrew by hisself."

My appetite returned after days of wrenching fear. I enjoyed a long, deep sleep that night. Two days later, Big D called again. I was finishing a plate of Momma's fantastic macaroni and cheese when he told me, "They got Willie and Dottie. It'll be in tomorra's paper. Poeleese say it was a murder suicide. He was shot in the head and her head was cut off. I think he cut her head off, then the numbers people got 'im."

I thought, *So Wicked Willie wasn't immortal like he thought he was.* "What happened to the money?" I asked my long-winded drug buddy.

"Who knows? Maybe the cops took it. I know I ain't got it."

After twice narrowly avoiding death at the hands of hired killers, any person with common sense would have walked away from the gangster life and never looked back. I lacked common sense, was still addicted to that lifestyle and believed I'd always come out on top. I was a brainless wonder on course to ending my life far too soon. An old joke went, "Live fast, die young and leave a good looking corpse," but I accepted it as Gospel truth. Was it the drugs that made me think that way? If stupidity were a crime, I would have been sentenced to life without parole.

When discharged from the hospital, the doctors told me, "Stay off your feet as much as possible or you'll rip the stitches out." Like a dummy, I didn't follow their orders and continued playing the wrong game for the cards I had been dealt.

I had been planning to rob a gas station before the mishap with my pistol and knew when the business would have the most cash on hand. All I needed was someone with a car. Big D said he knew where he could get one, but didn't want to go in the station with me. I said, "That's cool. All you hafta do is take me over to the place and just stay in the car. I'll go in and get the money."

Big D pulled up at my house in a Chevy Impala convertible with the top up. I recognized the car. It belonged to his older brother, Harry. Big D's brother was a tough dude who shaved his head, wore a Fu Manchu and worked at a GM plant. I was surprised Harry let his brother use the car because the only thing he loved more than his convertible was fishing.

I asked my accomplice, "What your brother doin' tonight?"

"Up in Canada fishin'."

I thought, *So Harry let 'im use the car while he was away.* In my state of stupidity, the possibility of someone taking down the license number of the Chevy convertible and getting Big D's brother in trouble never entered my mind.

Arriving at the gas station, I showed Big D where to park and got out of the Impala rag top. Not bothering with crutches, I limped into the office, stuck my handgun in the manager's face, grabbed a cloth bag filled with cash, came out and found the motor mouth and convertible gone.

I chose to escape through a field next to the station. Money fell out of the bag as I clumsily tried to run with an orthopedic pad on my right foot. I popped my stitches open and my foot started bleeding badly. Under a cloak of darkness, I somehow made it to a friend's house, leaving behind a trail of blood and paper currency. Neither the cops nor anyone at the gas station caught up with me, but Big D did. He offered an excuse. "My brother was lookin' for his ride and caught me with it."

"Ya mean ya didn't borrow it from him?"

"Nah, just took it. He come back from fishin' sooner'n expected. Made me give 'im the keys, got behind the wheel and drove straight home with his buddy followin'. I was lucky he didn't beat the brakes off me. Oh, by the way, my man, I still want my cut."

I gave him two hundred bucks, and he was fine with that. It was tough for somebody as talkative as Big D, but he managed to keep his mouth shut. I ended up with eight hundred, which didn't last long with my hundred dollar-a-day drug habit,

My gunshot wound had to be stitched again, prolonging my recovery. I had done another senseless thing and should have been treated for madness or punished for badness. It was only through God's mercy I avoided arrest. I craved drugs but was also addicted to living on the edge, which in many ways was worse than being hooked on dope.

"My mom used to say, 'Junior, you can do anything you want. Whether it's good or whether it's bad, you can do anything in life that you want to do.'"

KATHY'S PLAN
TO SAVE ME

I was wearing out my welcome in my hometown. This was brought home to me when I tried to see my baby daughter, PaQuana. The child's mother, Althea, was staying at her aunt's house, so I walked there and rang the bell. Althea answered, and the look on her face told me I was the last person in the world she wanted to see. She asked, "What do YOU want?"

"Wanna see PaQuana," I replied.

Althea responded in her harshest tone, "You're a dope fiend and you're robbin' the neighborhood! I want nothin' to do with you and don't want you seein' PaQuana." She slammed the door in my face.

Tears filled my eyes. I had never been hurt so badly before and like a fool, turned to drugs for comfort. I would stop at nothing to get money for them. I was in the fierce grip of addiction and on a downward spiral.

It reached the point where I put my girlfriend in danger. I could manipulate her because I was the love of her life, and she would do anything for me. She knew about some of my criminal behavior and that I drank wine and occasionally cough syrup, but nothing about my taking heroin.

Kathy was frequently allowed to use her dad's '68 Cadillac Coupe de Ville. I talked her into driving around to find a place to rob. I disguised myself by wearing a sweater and hat belonging to her. As we rode around the city, nothing looked promising until I spotted a party store with a vacant parking space in front. I had my girlfriend turn around and park in front of the store. I entered the place, pointed a snub nose .38 at the woman behind the counter, got the money, made my exit and climbed into the backseat of the Caddy. Kathy made a u-turn while I lay curled up on the seat.

A half mile from the crime scene, we stopped for a red light and a police car pulled up behind us. My girlfriend said, "Cops are here. They're right on my back bumper."

I replied, "Don't turn 'round and look at 'em. Just act normal and relax. Whatever ya do, don't go over the speed limit."

She replied in a frightened little girl voice, "Okay, I'll try." She held the steering wheel in a death grip and her brow was furrowed. Kathy had been brought up in the right spirit, and being involved in a criminal act instigated by her moronic boyfriend with the police a heartbeat away scared her to death.

We were twenty-five minutes from her house and hit every red light along the way. Kathy's lips were moving, but she was whispering so softly I had to strain my ears. I made out enough words to realize she was praying. The police car remained right behind us until the last light before our destination, where they turned off onto another street. Once the cops were no longer around, I climbed into the front seat. As we drove to Kathy's house, she said, "That's the longest, scariest ride I've ever been on. I'm not goin' through that again."

When we pulled up at her place, she turned to me and said, "I promised God that if the police didn't stop us, I'd get you out of Pontiac. I love you, Pink, and if you stay here, you'll end up dead."

"What we gonna do?" I asked.

"I have a plan," she replied. "First, we're gonna get married, so we can live together in an honorable way. Once I graduate, we'll both join the Army. They have a 'Buddy Buddy Program' so husbands and wives can be together."

I went along with her wishes, thinking, *I can get outta Pontiac and start a new life." We went to the nearest recruiting office and spoke to a staff sergeant. He was very impressed with Kathy, but took an instant dislike to me. I was dressed stylishly and thought I made a great impression, but he saw through me. From his tone of voice, I could tell he thought I was a thug who had no business being in the company of my intended wife. He said, "Thomas, be here tomorrow morning at eight. You're going to be tested.*

When I showed up the following morning, the sergeant had me sit at a desk and take the Army intelligence test. After I finished, he immediately had me take a four-part GED. All the tests were timed, but there were no clocks around, so it was up to him to tell me when time was up. I got through the intelligence test, but was sunk by the GED. I ran out of time and wasn't able to complete the last section.

If I hadn't dropped out of school, thinking I would learn more in the cracks, crevices and shadowy corners of the city, I would have done much better. But I also believe the staff sergeant cheated by telling me I was out of time when I really wasn't. I didn't have a watch and had no way of knowing for sure, but I could tell the recruiter thought I was going to bring Kathy down and made sure she got in and I stayed out.

She was eighteen, but I was only seventeen when we talked to our parents about getting married. Michigan didn't allow anyone under twenty-one to marry without parents' permission. With all the trouble I had been in, Mom and Dad thought I wasn't mature enough and wouldn't give their consent. We drove to Beaver Falls, Pennsylvania, where we met the age requirements, and were married by a justice of the peace on June nineteenth, 1975. I was high on heroin during the ceremony... not the best way to start a marriage. Our wedding, my wife's high school graduation and her leaving for the Army all happened within a week. There was no time for a honeymoon before she was sent to basic training at Fort Jackson, near Columbia, South Carolina.

While Kathy was away, I continued living with my mother and father. I wasted my time hanging out in Ray's Poolroom, located near a busy intersection on Franklin Road. One evening, the street was packed with workers heading home from the General Motors plant. During a long traffic light, a motorist saw me standing in front of Ray's and called out to me. I recognized him. He was a neighbor whose son had played Little League baseball with me. I walked out into traffic and leaned into the passenger window of his car. He said, "Thought you supposed to be goin' to the Army, boy."

I began to explain, but the light changed and horns started honking. My choices were get out of the street or get run over. As I moved away from his car, the neighbor said, "Boy, you ain't nothin' and ain't never gonna be nothin'." His comment stung me and made me feel worthless. I wanted to prove him wrong but with my wife so far away, I felt like every last door was being slammed in my face.

Two days later, I got a call from Kathy. My bride said, "Pink, honey, I've finished basic training and made arrangements for you to join me." I was so happy, I felt like singing. She sent me a plane ticket for Columbia. I flew there and stayed in a guest house on the Army base. Realizing I had been given another chance at life, I became determined to kick my drug habit. I did it cold turkey. For four days, I vomited often, had the sweats, couldn't sit still and was too jittery to sleep soundly. I tossed and turned and at one point, found the only place I could sleep was under the bed. Once clean, I calmed down.

While staying in the guest house I felt like I was under a microscope, so I looked for other housing. I found a rooming house owned by a black woman named Anna Malloy who always wore scarves, indoors as well as outdoors. I paid her forty dollars a week for a roach infested ten by ten room with a dresser and a bed. There was a water fountain in the hall and a bathroom I shared with everyone else on my floor. A refrigerator in the dining room was used by everybody in the house. When I first saw the sleazy quarters, I thought, *Whaaat?* but it was all I could afford in that city.

In addition to renting rooms, Mrs. Malloy was a psychic and tarot card reader. People paying for advice from the woman with skin the color of a copper coin handled by many fingers were coming and going at all hours, some arriving by cab. She was also involved in voodoo. During my first day as her tenant, she said in an assuring tone, "Young fella, you'll be safe here. No boo hags'll ride ya in this place."

"What's a boo hag?" I asked.

"Worst thing ya can imagine. They're dead people who steal the living's skin and wear it like clothes. Without the skin, they'll burn up in the sun. They come into houses at night through cracks in walls and steal energy from people while they sleep. They need the energy to keep goin'. Once they steal it, you're dead."

"How they do that?"

"A boo hag'll sit on yo' chest and ride ya 'til all yo' energy is gone and then they'll hafta get back into their skin 'fore the sun come up. Don't worry. I've stopped 'em from gettin' in here."

"Howdja do it?"

"See all the things painted indigo blue? They can't stand that color."

Mrs. Malloy picked up a straw broom and said, "I keep these around 'cuz if a boo hag sees one, they'll stop and count every straw. Might take 'em so long, the sun'll come out and they'll burn up."

I had a hard time believing in boo hags but if they did exist, it was good to know I was protected. I was more afraid of Anna Malloy's son than any boo hag. He often came by to see his mother and would be riding in a limousine. Within two days of moving into Mrs. Malloy's rooming house, I heard it said her son was a major drug dealer. He didn't know about my history of drug usage and in my desire to remain clean, I wasn't about to tell him.

I felt great with the drugs completely out of my system and decided to go into Columbia. There were two main streets. Harden Street was where Benedict University, a black college with a basketball team, could be found. Hastings Boulevard was the place for drug trafficking. Choosing the untroubled side of town, I started playing basketball and hanging out with the students at Benedict. Being around them motivated me to go back to school. I began making plans and stayed clean for three months. Everything changed when my wife told me she was being posted to Fort Lewis, near Tacoma, Washington.

Military personnel received big discounts from Greyhound Bus Lines, so my wife and I decided to "ride the 'hound" to her new assignment. We were on buses for three and a half days, but it was the best we could afford.

I had a hundred dollars when we arrived on the West Coast. While Kathy reported for duty, I found a one-bedroom furnished apartment not far from the post and put down a ninety-dollar deposit. The next day, I began looking for work. Having been rejected by the Army, I followed my wife's suggestion and went to the huge Army base to apply for civilian jobs.

My first two interviews were terrible. When questioned about my work experience, my mind went blank and I groped for words. In the middle of my third interview, I felt my throat closing up and sat with a tension filled expression on my face. I finally got up from my chair and walked out on the man talking to me. I was seventeen years old and felt like a failure. I wondered if my being unreliable would be permanent and if drug usage had cost me my ability to gain knowledge.

I needed money to live and went back to the things I knew best. Drifting into the local drug scene, I began dealing fake cocaine out of the One Two Three Club near the Army base. It was a G.I. hangout on weekends and always packed on the first and fifteenth when soldiers were paid. I mixed BC Powder, an over the counter medication for colds, headaches and minor pains, with sugar and passed the concoction off as cocaine. It cost less than five bucks to make and I could sell a gram for a hundred. I was taking insane to the membrane chances. I was too young to be allowed in the club, risked retaliation from those dealing real drugs, could have been stomped, beaten or shot by irate G.I.'s and had a wife in the Army who could have also gotten in trouble.

Skills learned from street hustlers in Pontiac helped me dupe the soldiers. Having been in so many of Pontiac's drug dens and pool rooms, I came across as an experienced dope hustler. No one suspected I was too young to be there. Soldiers thought my phony blow was real, and I made it sound real. Dealers from San Francisco were peddling the genuine article, but I hoodwinked the troops. "Don't listen to 'em," I'd say. "They sellin' garbage! I got what you want… da real deal, da fruit o'da loom." They believed me, and I was cleaning up on G.I. paydays until they finally figured out what I was up to. My wife knew I was getting money from somewhere, but was afraid to ask how I was doing it. It was strictly "Ask me no questions and I'll tell you no lies."

My ride on the gravy train ended abruptly. The only punishment I faced was everyone acting as though I didn't exist. Except for my wife, I found myself alone without any friends and had only myself to blame.

Life became more complicated when six months after arriving at Fort Lewis, Kathy became pregnant with our son, Pinklon III. She chose to leave the Army and received an honorable discharge. I had to get a job, so we decided to go to Seattle, where there were better prospects than Tacoma.

I wasted much of the money made from my hustle on my drug habit, but did buy a rattletrap car for a hundred and fifty bucks. It was a 1965 Buick LeSabre without shock absorbers, a radio, an emergency brake or turn signals. Its faulty transmission wouldn't shift to Park, and it had a rag in place of a gas cap.

The only piece of furniture we owned was a dresser. I tied it onto the Buick, and then my wife and I hit the interstate. We headed for the south part of Seattle, bouncing up and down as we rolled along.

MY BRIEF AMATEUR BOXING CAREER

My one step from a wrecking yard Buick LeSabre was totally unsuited for hilly Seattle. I had to make sure my wheels were properly turned either in or out whenever I parallel parked. If I didn't, the decrepit Buick would roll downhill and possibly damage another car. I had to signal using my left arm, and made quite a sight tooling around Seattle in my bouncing Buick, wearing an Army fatigue jacket acquired from a G.I.

On arriving in the Pacific Northwest metropolis, I was hired by Peerless Products on Michigan Street in south Seattle, a factory producing aluminum windows. I assembled windows and made sure everything was tight. Unfortunately, I was laid off after three months. In the meantime, I had become friends with Randy Caldwell and his wife Sherry, the property managers at the complex where my wife and I lived. They worked for Capretto and Clark Properties, and Randy helped me get hired by the real estate developer for seventy-five cents an hour more than what Peerless paid.

I was assigned to help renovate properties, and our rent was taken off the top of my pay. Things were fine for three months until the renovation work slowed up and I was laid off. I began to see what a mistake it had been to refuse going to school. High school dropouts are last to be hired and the first fired. Two layoffs in six months made me desperate for money.

Foolishly thinking I could support my young family by hustling, I went back into drug dealing and shooting dope. This only made things worse. We couldn't pay the rent, were evicted and forced to move into a housing project on Seattle's west side. I met a couple there named Terry and Karen Davis and tried to impress Terry by bragging, "I was on the boxing team at the Brewster Community Center in Detroit. Joe Louis came out of there. I won fifteen fights and had fifteen knockouts."

Terry believed me and said, "Man, that's pretty cool." Telling him the lie was a stupid way to win friends and influence people. I had never fought in a ring and seldom set foot in Detroit.

Two days later, Terry came to me and said, "I work in parks and recreation, and know a gym you oughta go to." He gave me the address and said, "Ask for an old guy named Joe West."

I had shot a speedball that day, a mixture of cocaine and heroin taken in one injection that produced the best high in the world of drugs. It also lured, lied to and often killed those who used it. In my dimwitted state, I didn't see where having the potent combination of narcotics in my system would make any difference. After all, I felt powerful, invincible and ready to take on a grizzly bear.

I jumped in my unsafe 1965 car and drove to the gym. Still under the influence of coke and smack, I walked in the place. The only person there was a skinny little black guy with sharp features, a high yaller complexion, a moustache, gray hair and glasses. He was sitting in a corner listening to a recording of Brazilian jazz pianist Eumir Diodato, reading a newspaper and smoking a long, thin brown cigarette. I recognized the brand as More. I stood at the front door and shouted, *"hey! Are you Joe West?"*

"How can I help you," he replied in a calm, low key manner.

"I'm Pinklon Thomas. I fought for Brewster Community Center in Detroit, same place Joe Louis come out of, and won fifteen straight with fifteen knockouts. I wanna fight."

"Oh, really?"

Joe got up, walked in a slow shuffling gait toward a closet resembling an armoire, opened the door and grabbed some boxing gloves. He tossed a pair to me and said, "Lemme see ya hit the bag." I didn't know how to pull the gloves on and lace 'em up, so he patiently put them on for me.

I started hitting the heavy bag, attacking it with both hands. The eighty-pound training device barely moved because I was punching only with my arms. After four minutes of feverish but futile activity, I was not only exhausted, but sick to my stomach. I ran out the back exit, hung over a railing and threw up in an alley. So much for the chemical courage and indomitable power I thought the speedball had given me.

When I staggered back into the gym, Joe West was rolling on the floor, pounding it and laughing so hard he gasped for breath. I asked, "What you laughin' at, old man?"

When finally able to speak, he said, "Ya never fought anybody. Might've fought in the streets, but ya never boxed in a ring. Go down to K-Mart and get some runnin' shoes and sweat pants. Then I'll show ya a few things."

I said, "All right. I'll be back."

A trip to K Mart wasn't needed because I still had shoes and sweat pants used for playing basketball. I packed them in my gym bag, headed to Joe West's the next day and began training. This time, there was no pistol in the bag.

Boxing was far above the raw brutality of street fighting. There were rules to be followed, skills to be mastered and strategies to be learned. The physical conditioning involved was the most demanding of all sports.

Joe told me I'd have to run three miles every day and hearing that, I knew I had to get in even better shape than basketball required. This meant laying off drugs, and I was determined to quit cold turkey, as I had in South Carolina. I did it by running until I threw up, then start running again and throwing up some more until the poison was out of my system. In the weeks to follow, my drug usage went down quite a bit, but I couldn't completely kick the habit.

I'm left handed and when street fighting as a kid, would lead with my right and use my left for power shots. Sixty-three-year-old Joe West had been in the fight game forty-seven years and knew all the ins and outs of the sport. He wanted to make the most effective use of my seventy-six-and-a-half-inch reach and powerful left hand by building my style of fighting around the left jab.

He converted me from a southpaw stance to fighting right handed. He explained, "There's two reasons for this. First, it's very hard to get fights for southpaws. Second, right handed fighters jab with their left. Your left hand is the more powerful one, and you could develop a jab that'll knock down a house. It'll give ya a big advantage."

I had another competitive advantage Bob Kaiser once pointed out to me: My killer instinct. I remember him saying, "Pink, you're usually a pretty nice guy but when ya flip the script and go into that other world, I can't go in there with ya. I have to wait until ya come back."

Joe's chief second was Jack Stafford, a Kenny Rogers lookalike who played the guitar. Stafford had begun teaching boxing at the Red Shield Community Center and later moved to the Del Ridge Community Center Gym. He helped me enormously by demonstrating proper execution of fundamentals. He taught me to push off the back leg, pivot with my feet, rotate my hips, snap my shoulders and put full weight into my punches. He also worked the punch mitts with me and helped develop my reflexes, peripheral vision, confidence and discipline. Jack was also a gold mine of good advice. He'd say, "Pink, you gotta control your own movements before you can control your opponent's movements."

Under Joe and Jack's guidance, I learned how to throw powerful jabs, hooks and uppercuts with my left hand, but still hadn't developed my right. I was using it for grabbing my opponent, tying them up and getting into a clinch. My right hand wasn't good for much more than waving, but my left was a force to be reckoned with. Joe West said, "When you connect with it, I hear a cannon or the crack of thunder."

Joe West's gym with its grunts heard from sparring boxers, squeaking of metal chains attached to heavy bags, smells of liniment, rat-tap-tap of jump ropes striking the floor and men shadow boxing became my second home. Joe was impressed with how quickly I picked things up. I was able to get a job with Goodwill Industries, sorting and cleaning up donated items. With both me and my wife working, our financial situation became stable.

Still not totally free of "illusions created and delusions invaded," I had a brief relapse into the gangster lifestyle because of a black dude I met at a K Mart. I was in front of him in a checkout line, and he was there with a woman. They made a good-looking couple. He was five eight and a hundred fifty. She was curvy, and both had big Afros not often seen in Seattle. He used a credit card to make a purchase large enough for the clerk to check a bulletin of invalid card numbers. She found his card on the list, kept it and went to get a manager. I looked at him and asked, "You all right, man?"

He looked back at me and nodded. Game recognizes game, and I knew he was trying to pull off a flimflam, but it wasn't working. Motioning with my head and eyes, I let him know I was going to my car. He left the woman and followed me out of the store. When he got outside, he began running and employees took up the chase. I started my car, pulled out of the parking lot and turned onto Del Ridge Way. The man with the Afro suddenly appeared from trees along the main road. I stopped the car, he jumped in and we took off.

We went to my place in south Seattle. My wife was at work, so we could talk freely. He told me his name was Jay and he sold dope for a supplier from Texas. This was a trigger that pulled me back into the drug game. I was still using, was making minimum wage and needed more money. I began selling drugs with Jay and brought in a hundred a day, cold cash. It was a way to support my heroin habit and bring in a little extra.

This wasn't enough for Jay. He wanted much more and began talking about ripping off a stash house that moved a lot of mescaline and marijuana. The day he decided to pull the job, he drove to my place, parked his car and then had me come out to see what was in the trunk. There was a sawed off and a pistol. He said, "Come on, man, let's go right now. We gotta do this thang!"

I replied, "Hold up, man. Let's go to the gym. You can hang out with me. I'm tellin' ya, my man, if things take off for me, I'm takin' ya with me."

Jay's response was, "Man, you must be outta yo' mind! Got fantasy in yo' head!"

I had a bad feeling and said, "I ain't goin." Before he could say another word, I started walking away.

He hollered, *"You crazy!"* got behind the wheel, put his car in Drive and took off. It was reported on the news that night Jay had been busted. He ended up getting eight to fifteen. Jay's sad end was enough to cure my addiction to the gangster lifestyle. I still had my drug problem to contend with, but had taken a big step forward. I finally got it into my thick skull that all my skin folk are not my kinfolk and I had to segregate myself from criminals. Any thoughts of getting over on "The Man" had to come to an end. Thanks to God's mercy, the only time I had been caught by the police was when I was fourteen and they found the bag of weed on me.

I was only nineteen years old, had shown good speed when competing in track and had excelled in AAU basketball. I thought about trying out for the Seattle Supersonics NBA team or the NFL's Seattle Seahawks but not having competed in college sports and with a family to support, I figured boxing was the way to go.

Though only a raw newcomer still unsure of my skills, Old Joe West encouraged me to enter the Tacoma Golden Gloves held at the Tacoma Sports Arena in January, 1978. I was matched in the heavyweight class against Tommy Thomas, an inmate at the Washington State Penitentiary in Walla Walla. I lasted the three rounds, wasn't knocked down, showed some power in my right hand for a change and filled my opponent's face with leather, but the judges awarded the decision to the convict. While showering afterwards, I said, "That's alright, Tommy, I'm gonna get ya at the Seattle Golden Gloves."

He replied, "No you're not, Pink. You hit too hard. I'm goin' down to light heavyweight."

After emerging from the locker room, I was introduced by Joe West to Roland Jankelson, who had expressed an interest in becoming my manager when I was ready to turn pro. He came from a wealthy family. His father, Dr. Bernard Jankelson, was a renowned dentist, known as "Dr. J." Just as Julius "Dr. J" Erving was considered one of the greatest basketball players of all time, Roland's father was regarded as one of the best dentists in history. He was an expert on jaw malfunctions, introduced neuromuscular dentistry and was celebrated for the perfect bites he built for his patients. He also invented the Myomonitor, an electronic muscle stimulator he sold to many prosthodontists.

Roland became even wealthier than his father through real estate. He also invested ten grand as a minority stockholder in the Portland Trailblazers when they were brought into the NBA as an expansion team. After the Trailblazers won the NBA World Championship in

1977, his ten-thousand-dollar investment was worth six hundred grand. Everything Jankelson touched seemed to turn to gold.

Always well-groomed and in stylish clothes, Roland wore glasses, had a habit of walking fast and was always chasing the next big thing. He had hit a jackpot with basketball. Perhaps he might do as well with a heavyweight fighter not quite twenty years old. With a wife and infant son to support, I hoped the man with the golden touch might work his magic for me. Roland ended our first meeting by saying, "We'll talk more after the Golden Gloves are over."

The week before the Seattle Golden Gloves was filled with misfortune. Jack Stafford, who contributed so much to my development as a fighter, suffered an injury while working at his full-time job on a garbage truck. His right hand was caught in the machinery and he lost two fingers. He wouldn't be able to work with me for a while.

Two days before my first fight in the Seattle tournament, Joe West took me to a downtown gym where I sparred with two white dudes who were battle hardened pro boxers: "Ibar the Sailor Man" Arrington and Boone Kirkman. Ibar had fought heavyweight champ Larry Holmes and was getting ready for an eight rounder. He had an excellent left jab, a great right hand and a remarkable chin. Boone was a former tavern brawler and street fighter from the blue-collar suburb of Renton, Washington. Both were household words to Seattle fight fans.

I had never sparred more than three rounds against quality heavyweights. After three rounds with Arrington, I was struggling to catch my breath and gasped to Joe West, "I'm shot. I'm done. Can't go another round."

Joe Torres, the owner of the gym, was managing both Arrington and Kirkman. Torres became upset about the sparring session ending so soon. He whined to Joe West, "Aw man, give us one more round."

My light skinned, sixty-three-year-old trainer said to me, "C'mon, Pink, just give 'em one more round."

Reluctantly, I replied, "Okay, man. All right, I'll do it."

Halfway through the round, I was done… completely out of gas. Normally, I could study a punch coming at me and pull my head out of harm's way at the last instant. This time, I was exhausted, couldn't get away from what I saw coming, was hit on the left side of my chin and fell back on the ropes. Despite wearing protective head gear, pain ripped through places near my left ear and jaw.

Just then, the timer went "ding" to end the round. I felt a sharp, stabbing pain and said to Joe West, "My jaw's killin' me."

"Come here. Open your mouth." I opened it for him. He asked, "Can you close it?" I clenched my teeth and said, "Yeah."

"Go get ya some Super Bubble Gum and chew it. You'll be all right."

My first tournament bout was against a six two, two hundred forty-three pounder known as "Big Blue." He had jet black skin and looked like Sonny Liston. He was also a convict, like Tommy Thomas, who I fought in Tacoma. After the fight, he would be taken back to the state prison in Monroe, Washington. He outweighed me by fifty pounds, but my rapid fire left jab caused him to bleed from the nose and I was awarded the decision. I was happy about my first boxing victory, but my jaw was killing me.

I told Joe about my jaw and asked, "How'm I gonna fight tonight?"

"Don't worry, I'm gonna take ya over to my house. I'll put ice on your jaw, feed ya and ya can rest up."

I stretched out on his couch with an ice pack on my jaw and went to sleep. Joe watched a football game while I napped and woke me when dinner was ready. His wife, Martha, had cooked a pot roast with potatoes and carrots which smelled delicious and made my mouth water, but it was too painful for me to bite or chew. Joe said to his wife, "Look up in that cabinet. There's a Cup-A-Soup. He should be able to eat that." I had the soup and drank juice from the meat, potatoes and vegetables. After the skimpy meal, I went back to the couch and slept for another hour and a half.

When I woke up, we got in Joe's car and left for the Seattle Center Arena. Along the way, he stopped at a drug store. I asked, "What we stoppin' here for?"

"Don't worry about it."

Arriving at the arena, Joe wrapped my hands then said, "Hey, Pink, take out your mouth guard."

I removed it. He positioned an aspirin next to a tooth where my jaw was hurting. He spread medicine on the bottom of my mouth guard, placed it back in my mouth and told me to bite down. It was the nastiest stuff I ever tasted.

I went into the ring to face Big Randy Nelson, a local white hope, for the Pacific Northwest Golden Gloves heavyweight title. He was six-two and two-hundred-forty-three pounds. The crowd went crazy when a spotlight shined on him. At the opening bell, he began fighting dirty and mauled me by pushing his head against my chest and head butting my chin. I was lucky he didn't draw blood. He forced me against the ropes and I hit him with a right. He went down and the referee said, "Go to a neutral corner." I did as I was told, and the referee began his count. Randy got up on the count of eight. I thought, *Oh God, why does he hafta get up?*

Big Randy bared his teeth, came at me again and tried to cut my face with the laces of his gloves. I fell back on the ropes once more. This time, I hit him with a left hook and he went down again. The referee ordered, "Go to a neutral corner," and then began counting. Once again, the big white heavyweight got up at the count of eight.

The dirty fighter with a fifty-pound weight advantage rushed at me. I fell back, heard Joe West bellow, *"Get off the ropes!"* then hit Big Randy with a left hook, right hand combination. He seemed to float upwards before crashing to the canvas. The crowd was in an uproar. I went to a neutral corner without needing to be told and the referee started counting. I looked at my opponent laying on his back and thought, "Lord, they can count to a hundred, but this guy ain't gettin' up."

Rather than celebrating with Joe, I had him take me straight home because my jaw was so painful. I woke up at three thirty in the morning, looked in the mirror and saw my jaw had swollen to the size of an orange. My wife insisted, "Go to the hospital."

The diagnosis was a broken jaw, and a specialist was called in to perform emergency surgery. My jaw was wired, forcing me to get nourishment through a straw. I was on liquids for eight weeks, which seemed like an eternity. I put every type of food imaginable through a blender in order to keep my weight and strength up. When the doctor removed the wires, he discovered a tooth had split. It was removed and my jaw rewired. I was on liquids for another four weeks and lost twenty-one pounds, dropping down to one seventy-two. I wasn't big enough to fight as a heavyweight.

My victory over Big Randy Nelson qualified me to fight in the National Golden Gloves, held in Hawaii, but my broken jaw and resulting weight loss prevented me from competing in the finals. Greg Page, another heavyweight who converted from a southpaw, wound up winning the national title. He entered the professional ranks through the front door and was touted as possessing the power punch, hand speed and chin to beat any contender for the world title. I had to enter professional boxing through the back door.

I knew nothing about the boxing business. I agreed to provide a small amount of financial support so that Pinklon could train and turn pro. Soon after, I became his manager, and the rest is history.

— Roland Jankelson

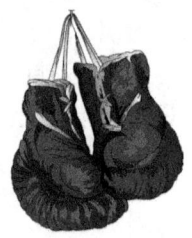

TURNING PRO

Roland Jankelson had dollar signs for eyes and hoped to make a killing through pro boxing, just as he had with the Portland Trailblazers. He signed me to a management contract in 1978, when I was twenty and had fought only three times as an amateur. I was given a three thousand dollar signing bonus, and Joe West took a thousand of it for being my trainer. Roland also paid for having my jaw taken care of and arranged a job for me, working on a small assembly line that produced his father's Myomonitors. It felt great to be rewarded for honest work.

I spent my time at the job sitting at a work bench and soldering wires for eight dollars an hour. I had never soldered before, but quickly picked up the technique. Dr. J treated me like a son and devised a custom fitted mouth guard for me at no cost. It offered tremendous protection for my twice wired jaw and if not for that mouthpiece, I wouldn't have been able to continue fighting.

Roland was to receive a third of my net purses, Joe West would get ten percent as my trainer and I would keep fifty-six and two-thirds. I was the first fighter Roland managed. He was not a boxing man and looked at the sport the same way he looked at real estate, thinking he could manage me the same way he managed property. In time, he learned property doesn't talk back, while fighters do. Roland has since gone on to manage many professional boxers and became very knowledgeable about the fight game.

Running three miles in the early morning, performing an exacting job of soldering from nine to five and training for two hours after work was not the way for a professional fighter with championship aspirations to prepare. I had a heart to heart discussion with my manager and explained that in order to get the most return for his investment, I would have to be training full time. I said, "My goal is to become a world champion, and I have a family to support," then went over our living expenses. Roland spoke in a careful, schoolmasterly way and agreed to pay me a stipend of fifteen hundred dollars a month. It was not an advance, so it wouldn't count against any of my purses. By this time, my wife was working at Equitable Life and Casualty Insurance, so we were doing pretty well. We were able to buy a two-year-old Cadillac Fleetwood.

The realtor moonlighting as a fight manager set up a promotional group called Round One Productions by gathering eight investors who chipped in two grand apiece. I was sent to Jimmy Montoya's Olympic Gym in Los Angeles for eight weeks of training to ready me for my professional debut. The gym occupied a faded yellow brick building that was originally a place where girls could be hired for a dime a dance. It got its name because it was across from the legendary Olympic Auditorium.

I received good news on my return to Seattle when I was greeted by Jack Stafford. He had recovered from his on the job injury which cost him two fingers and would be able to help me train and be the second man in my corner.

I also had the advantage of being able to spar "Laughing Larry" Frazier, a six four and a half, two hundred forty pounder who had been one of Muhammad Ali's sparring partners. He was called "Laughing Larry" because of his fearsome facial expressions when in the ring. He had an eighty-inch reach, three and a half inches longer than mine. The San Francisco born heavyweight had won seven of his ten pro fights, and one of his victims was heavyweight contender Mike "Hercules" Weaver.

Two of Frazier's losses were to six-foot five-inch, two-hundred-forty-pound Leroy Jones.

The massive New York born Jones, who had once been a defensive end on Grambling University's football team, moved to Denver after multimillionaire Bill Daniels put him under contact. Leroy was preparing to fight Mike Weaver for the NABF heavyweight title. I was sparring with both Laughing Larry and Leroy. I held my own with the two far more experienced fighters because I realized winning a boxing match was very much like solving problems in school. I had to learn the right methods and wouldn't be able to do it if I was the rebellious knucklehead I had been as a kid. Joe West and Jack Stafford were my teachers and Larry Frazier and Leroy Jones were my tutors. This time, I paid attention in class.

My first pro fight presented an unusual challenge. Most professional boxers start out with four round fights in small clubs, but my debut was scheduled for six rounds at the Seattle Center Arena. My opponent was far more experienced. Ken Arlt of Portland, Oregon was six two, weighed two-forty-three and was similar in size to Big Randy Nelson, but not the dirty fighter Nelson was. Counting both amateur and pro bouts, Arlt had thirty fights under his belt, while I had only three amateur outings. I nearly went nuts waiting in the dressing room, my nerves were about to kill me, my stomach became upset and I vomited. Our fight lasted the scheduled six rounds and I won a split decision. With all my prefight jitters, it was one of the toughest bouts I ever had. Never again was I that nervous before a fight.

After my successful debut, I won eight straight, all by knockout. The only fight outside Seattle was in Billings, Montana, where I faced forty-three-year-old Elmo "Tex" Henderson. Elmo was a slick as lard and twice as greasy veteran of the ring whose claim to fame was facing Muhammad Ali in a two round exhibition staged at San Antonio, Texas during October, 1972. Henderson also served as a sparring partner for

George Foreman when Foreman fought Ali in Zaire. I couldn't lay a glove on the wily veteran until he ran out of gas in the fourth round. My tank was almost empty as I sat in the corner before that round, but Joe West said, "He's tired, Pink, he's tired. You gonna get to him." Joe was right, and I knocked him out. I later made use of Tex' ring savvy by hiring him as a sparring partner.

My unbeaten streak put my parents' minds at ease. I didn't find out until later, but they were very worried that if I began my pro career with a series of losses, I might become depressed and go back to my criminal ways. As long as I was winning, they were at peace knowing I was making money legitimately.

Upon returning to Seattle from the fight in Montana, I learned Jankelson had arranged a ten-round bout with Leroy Caldwell at Vegas' Silver Slipper in July, 1979. Joe West was angry because it was done without his input. Old Joe didn't think I was ready for Caldwell, a one hundred-ninety-two-pounder with a record of eight wins, a loss, two draws and five knockouts. His best performance was fighting heavyweight contender Trevor Berbick to a draw. Leroy had also served time in a penitentiary from the age of fifteen until he was twenty-two, and convicts stay in shape and come to fight.

The atmosphere in my dressing room before the fight was gloomy. Joe wrapped my hands, and then lit up a More cigarette. Roland, who always walked fast, nervously paced back and forth. Jack Stafford was quiet as a mouse. No one said a word to me. I thought, *I feel like I'm at a funeral... mine.* I had to do something to brighten the mood, so I broke the depressing silence by saying, "You guys act like you're goin' to a funeral. I'm gonna knock this chump out!" I put Joe West in front of me and placed my hands on his shoulders. I told my other two handlers, "Jack, you get behind me. Roland, you walk alongside us." That's how we came out of the dressing room and made our way through the crowd.

I was an unknown wearing a pink robe with "Think Pink" on the back and entered the ring to thunderous chants sending shivers up my spine. They were hollering, "LEROY! LEROY! LEROY!" I was facing the home favorite and if I expected to win, I had to knock him out because it's next to impossible to win a decision against a hometown hero. It was a tough fight. Caldwell was in control at the beginning and rumbled me several times but at two minutes and forty-eight seconds of the tenth round, I hit Leroy with a right-hand power shot to his chin. He flipped like a bucket and couldn't get off the canvas. The janitors had to sweep him up. I won by a knockout, but broke the fourth metacarpal bone in my left hand.

After my upset victory, I had ten wins, no losses and nine straight knockouts. Roland was swamped with offers of fights for me, but my hand needed to heal. My manager had no knowledge of boxing and was relying on opinions from people no better qualified than him. Having put twenty thousand of his money into me, in addition to the sixteen grand from his investors, Roland was anxious to get the dough back. He proposed I fight Jimmy Young, the cleverest heavyweight around. I didn't want to take the fight because I didn't feel ready. I needed to find out more about Young, so I called Young's trainer, George Benton. Benton said, "No, heck no. Jimmy's got a streak of five straight knockouts. You don't need to fight him now."

After I refused to fight Jimmy Young, Roland wanted me to take on Ron Lyle. I wasn't ready for him either. With eight years more experience than me, he had fought Muhammad Ali, George Foreman and Earnie Shavers. Lyle possessed a five knuckled bomb for a right hand and was regarded as one of the hardest punching heavyweights of the 1970s. I told my manager, "I'm goin' back to Michigan, let my hand heal and visit my family."

*"It's only through the grace of God I survived the crazy times
and the mission I was on.
I get chill bumps thinking about it today.
I did some very, very stupid stuff.
I got lucky, I was blessed."*

I ATTRACT A NUMBERS RACKETEER'S INTEREST

Arriving in Pontiac, I sought out some of the guys I'd known and excitedly told them about my new career. I said, "I'm a professional heavyweight boxer now. I'm 10 and 0 with nine straight knockouts." Their reaction wasn't what I expected.

A cat named Jesse, who was on the Junior Chaparrals with me, said, "Aw man, it's always the same thing with ya. Ya coulda gone somewhere in basketball and didn't. You're never goin' anywhere and you'll end up back here with us."

I replied, "No, man, I'm gonna be champion of the world." Jesse thought that was the funniest thing he'd ever heard and laughed so hard he gasped for breath and held his ribs. I never forgot the sound of his laughter, and it became a motivating force in my life. Whenever I was tempted to slacken off in training or quit boxing, the memory of Jesse's laughter restored my determination.

My old pals didn't believe in me, but Bob Kaiser did. Roland Jankelson had supplied me with eight-millimeter films of the Leroy Caldwell fight and a couple of my other pro bouts. I brought the films with me when I returned to Pontiac and loaned them to Bob, who took them to two men he had grown up with: Elbert Hatchett and Fred Corr. Elbert and Fred watched the films and when he saw my left jab in action, Corr instantly smelled money. He was even wealthier than Roland Jankelson and had the means to showcase me in New York City, Philadelphia and Atlantic City in hopes of obtaining fights for huge purses.

Freddie Corr achieved his wealth through illegal gambling. He was Pontiac's numbers king, earning fifteen million a year from the wildly popular racket that allowed working stiffs to win five hundred bucks by betting a dollar. Fred became big by not cheating those who played and paying off the same night a number hit. Bernie Muldrew, who I had been accused of killing when sixteen, was one of Corr's numbers runners.

Corr was born in 1931, graduated from Pontiac Central High in 1948 and had been operating his policy racket for thirty years. He was five-nine and one seventy-five, had coffee colored skin, wore his hair cut short, had a thick moustache and dressed conservatively. He wasn't athletic, and never played sports. His game was numbers, and the cash he accumulated was his scoreboard.

The numbers mastermind was never busted or raided because he paid off corrupt police and city officials. He avoided problems with the IRS by stating his occupation as "professional gambler," and making twenty-five-thousand-dollar quarterly self-employment payments. Freddie once said, "As long as you pay Caesar, Caesar will let you matriculate, but you can't get too flamboyant with him." He had a million-dollar home in Bloomfield Hills, but lived a very quiet, low key life, well under law enforcement's radar. He seldom drove, and Bob Kaiser often chauffeured him around.

Elbert Hatchett was very supportive of Fred's idea and drew up a management contract at no charge. This was a very generous act because Elbert was one of the most successful lawyers in the nation. A wealthy attorney who appeared in court with shoulder length hair and stylish clothes, he represented the NAACP and won a landmark desegregation case which led to forced busing. He also won a twenty-one-million-dollar worker's comp claim for Detroit Lions star Billy Sims.

Corr's plan included hiring Bob Kaiser to be my trainer and traveling companion. When Freddie made the offer to Bob, my old basketball coach hedged, saying, "I don't know, man, I've got so many years in at the plant." Bob was doing pretty well for himself. He had three jobs, working for GM, the city and the school district. The numbers king knew he would have to come up with an additional incentive.

Bob often visited Freddie at his home, so Corr asked him to come over, saying, "There's something I want to show you." When Bob arrived, his old friend took him into a room, pulled out a wicker suitcase and opened it. The suitcase contained a million in cash. Corr said, "I can guarantee you won't lose a dime working for me. I can match whatever you're making now or are ever gonna make. As a matter of fact, I'll deposit two hundred thousand in an account under your name. If anything ever happens between me, you and Pinky to end the arrangement, then it's yours. Until then, don't touch it."

Bob said, "That's okay, Fred. We grew up together. I know you'll take care of me."

I had been talking to Emanuel Steward and Prentiss Byrd, who were with the Kronk Boxing Team in Detroit that had produced world champs Thomas Hearns and Hilmer Kenty. They were very interested in meeting me, but my old basketball coach proposed placing my boxing career in the hands of Fred Corr. Bob Kaiser said, "Freddie's a gangster, but he's also a good neighbor, somethin' like Robin Hood. Your mom and dad knew both Freddie and me as kids. When we were growin' up, we weren't allowed into the mainstream of society, 'The Man's reality.' We had to create our own reality. Fred did it by participating in a second economy. Several heavyweights have been managed by those in the numbers racket. Joe Louis' managers were numbers guys, and so was Don King." Bob convinced me Corr was somebody I could trust and would look out for my best interests.

I signed the contract Elbert Hatchett drew up. According to its terms, I would keep seventy five percent of my net earnings from purses. Bob Kaiser received ten percent of the net and the numbers racketeer's share was fifteen percent. In addition, Corr agreed to give me five thousand to cover the cost of my family's relocation from Seattle to Utica, Michigan, pay me a stipend of fifteen hundred a month and cover the rent on a townhouse in Utica for a year.

TRIP TO THE BIG APPLE AND SOME LAST-MINUTE MATCHMAKING

F red Corr knew he had to get Roland Jankelson out of the picture, so he flew to Seattle with Bob Kaiser and me. Fred intended to buy my contract from Roland. A meeting was held in the conference room of Jankelson's real estate firm.

Roland looked like he stepped off the cover of GQ Magazine. Bob and I wore suits but for some strange reason, the numbers king chose to dress like a farmer. He wore heavy work boots, bib overalls and a plaid flannel lumberjack shirt. Fred Corr made an underwhelming impression on Roland, even though he had more money than the realtor, I suspect Jankelson didn't think Corr had enough to buy any fighter's contract.

By then, Jankelson and his partners had sunk seventy grand into me, but Fred offered him thirty thousand. Roland said, "It appears you have no idea what an unbeaten heavyweight is worth." He was about to get up from the conference table and end the meeting, when Fred replied, "I'll go to forty thousand."

Roland's response was, "I won't sell for less than one hundred thousand dollars." End of conversation and end of the trip to the Pacific Northwest.

When the three of us returned to Pontiac, Fred sent Bob Kaiser and me to New York City. We stayed at the Statler Hilton on 34th Street across from Madison Square Garden. Bob and I were there eight weeks, but it was far from a vacation. Each morning, we ran five miles along Central Park's hills, past benches, boulders and a lake. I also worked out twice a day at the 42nd Street Gym. I was looking good in the workouts, making a speed bag sing a song, and word quickly spread. "There's a new champ in town."

I was interviewed by The Ring magazine for their New Faces section. I said to the reporter, "I'm the fastest heavyweight in the world. Nine straight kayos tells you I'm playin' with more than popguns. All I want to do is train and fight. I want to win the heavyweight title with less total fights than any man in history."

Fred knew he would have to settle up with Roland Jankelson at some point and felt he needed help in carrying an expense that might exceed a hundred grand, so he sent us to meet Dick Gidron, a successful black new car dealer. Gidron owned a Cadillac dealership in the Bronx doing forty-five million a year in business and sold cars to George Steinbrenner and New York mayor David Dinkins. He also had three homes and a thirty-six-foot yacht. In addition, he was chairman of the Bronx Democratic Committee and close friends with Congressman Charles Rangel and activist Al Sharpton. Gidron was physically much bigger than I expected. He stood six feet four and weighed well over two hundred pounds, but wasn't flabby. He had a round face, wore glasses and was bald on top, with black Brillo-like hair along the sides.

After our visit to Gidron's dealership, Fred Corr called the car dealer and discussed his buying a piece of my contract. Dick sounded interested, but wanted to think it over. In the meantime, Bob Kaiser took me to Philadelphia, and I began training at Joe Frazier's Gym.

The first day we walked in, no one was working out. I asked, "Who cleared the streets?"

An old timer said, "Man, where you been? You didn't know HBO is holdin' their first all heavyweight card in A.C. next weekend? In case you don't know,

A.C. means Atlantic City."

I started shadow boxing in the empty gym. As I worked up a good sweat, I looked at the faces on a poster advertising the HBO Young Heavyweights boxing show at the Atlantic City Convention Center. I imagined what I would do against everyone on the card, all of them Don King fighters, thinking, "If one of 'em pulls out, I'll be ready."

With my mind on Atlantic City, I trained intensively. Each morning, Bob and I went on a five and a half mile run along East River Drive which always ended at the Philadelphia Museum and the statue of Rocky Balboa. We made an odd-looking pair of runners, with me tall enough to eat pie off the top of Bob's head. I would be in Smokin' Joe Frazier's gym from three in the afternoon until five thirty in the evening. Joe won a gold medal at the 1964 Tokyo Olympics and became world heavyweight champion in 1970 by knocking out Jimmy Ellis. Smokin' Joe won the title while Muhammad Ali was in exile for his refusal to be inducted into the military during the Vietnam War. The following year, 1971, Frazier and Ali faced each other in Madison Square Garden, with Frazier being awarded the decision after fifteen hard fought rounds. Joe lost his crown to George Foreman in 1973 and later lost twice to Ali. His rivalry with The Greatest is acknowledged as the finest in boxing annals. The man who had risen from being a Beaufort, South Carolina vegetable picker and church janitor to a legendary heavyweight champion graciously welcomed me, and it was inspiring to be around him.

The Friday before the Young Heavyweights show, we rented a car, drove to the Resorts Hotel in Atlantic City and checked in. It was eight thirty at night when Bob and I went down to the casino area and began playing roulette. At eleven forty-five, I heard a page, "Will Pinklon Thomas please report to the front desk?" but continued playing.

At three in the morning, I was ahead and paged again. This time, Bob answered the page for me. The voice on the other end of the line was fight promoter Ronald "Butch" Lewis. He spoke in a rat-a-tat-tat staccato style reminiscent of Walter Winchell and asked Bob, "Are you Pinklon Thomas' manager?"

"I'm his trainer. I can get hold of his manager if you need him."

"You guys wanna take a fight?"

"Who do you want him to fight?"

"Bobby Jordan. Was supposed to fight Randolph 'Tex' Cobb, but Tex came down with tendonitis."

Bob said, "Lemme talk to his manager and get right back to you."

My friend and trainer found me at the roulette wheel and said, "Come up to the room with me. It's important." When we entered our hotel room, Bob headed straight for his copy of the current Ring Magazine Record Book. He said, "Pink, Butch Lewis wants you to fight Bobby Jordan in place of Tex Cobb."

I asked, "What do you know 'bout the guy?"

Bob had been thumbing through the reference book and located information on Jordan. He said, "Jordan's from Virginia Beach, Virginia. He weighs one ninety-five and has a reach five inches shorter than you. He's not as tall as you, so we've got advantages over him in a few areas. I think we should take the fight."

Bob and I returned to the casino and met with Butch Lewis, who was dressed in an outfit that had become his trademark. He was wearing a white tuxedo and tie, but no shirt.

Bob said, "We'll take the fight if the price is right. How much was Tex Cobb supposed to get?"

Butch replied, "Forty-five hundred, but we can't give your guy that much."

"Why not?"

"Randy Cobb's ranked number ten."

Bob turned to me and said, "Go on up to the room and take a nap." He later told me what happened during the negotiations. Bob looked Lewis in the eye and told the promoter, "I'm five foot two, and I could whup Cobb. Pinky's better'n Randy."

Butch Lewis chuckled and said, "You don't seem to be afraid of anybody and just might be able to whup Randy. Okay, Pinky gets forty-five hundred."

It took an hour to close the deal, and Bob woke me with the news at four thirty in the morning. The forty-five-hundred-dollar purse was my biggest up to that point. We called Freddie Corr and he flew in for the fight. When the referee stopped the fight in the fifth round and awarded me a TKO, Bobby Jordan had a knot as big as a golf ball under his right eye.

I heard Bob Kaiser shout, *"The pink panther's on the loose!"* HBO's coverage of my victory landed me on the radar screens of everyone in boxing.

"Pinklon Thomas is a great fighter," said Holmes, the International Boxing Federation's champion, "and one of these days he's going to be a great champion — when I leave."

— Larry Holmes

A VULNERABLE GREEN PRO

F ollowing my win over Bobby Jordan, Dick Gidron agreed to throw in with Freddie Corr. My contract was rewritten, with the terms changed to sixty percent for me, ten percent for Bob Kaiser and thirty percent to be divided between Corr and Gidron. We celebrated the new arrangement with dinner at Sardi's in New York. Bob Kaiser ordered matzo ball soup.

Seated across the table from my trainer, six-foot four-inch Gidron said, "Hey, Bobby, whatcha got there?"

"Got some matzo ball soup."

The Cadillac dealer replied, "Hey that looks pretty good."

Gidron picked up a spoon, reached across the table with one of his long arms, dipped it into the bowl Bob was eating from and took part of a matzo ball and some of the soup. Bob looked at me and I looked at him. After dinner was over, we went for a walk. Bob said, "No, Pink, we can't mess with that Gidron dude. Man, he's one greedy son of a gun. Didja see him eat the food right outta my bowl? No tellin' what he might do to us if we get him angry." I began to wonder what I had gotten myself into, but then thought, "Sixty percent is still better'n the fifty-six and two-thirds I had with Roland."

By mid-December, 1979, Fred Corr had sunk twenty thousand dollars in me. He called and said he was making a trip to New York so he could discuss something important with me. I looked forward to the meeting. I had been wondering when my first fight under the new contract would take place and hoped I would be told one had been arranged.

I met with Corr in his hotel suite. We were both seated at a small table when Freddie reached into a briefcase and brought out a banded stack of C-notes and a contract. He said, "This money's for you. You and your family can have a nice Christmas."

"How much is there," I asked.

"Five grand."

"What do I hafta do for it?"

He placed the contract in front of me and said, "Just sign this paper where the X is.

The money's a Christmas bonus."

I quickly read over the document. It said I would be giving fifty percent of my gross purses to Fred and Dick. I asked, "What about the contract I already have?"

"Oh, this one is much better for you," answered the numbers king. "The old contract divvied up the net. This one cuts up a bigger pie. Anyone knows half a big pie is much better than sixty percent of a small one."

"What about Bob Kaiser," I asked.

Corr replied, "Oh, you pay him out of your end, but we split all other expenses fifty-fifty."

I should have told him I wanted time to think it over and then showed the new contract to Elbert Hatchett. As a twenty-one-year-old lacking formal education, all I could think was, "Gonna have a Merry Christmas with five G's ta spend." I foolishly signed the paper and took the five grand. The numbers king and the Cadillac dealer had goosed a green kid.

When I showed Bob Kaiser my new contract, he just shook his head and said, "What's done is done. You gotta deal with it and keep it movin'."

"Ya sound like ya think it's a bad idea," I said. "What's wrong with it?"

"Well, I worked in a factory, and learned the difference between gross and net. See, what ya did was sign up for a smaller portion, plus you're gonna pay me outta your portion and also pick up half the expenses. If Elbert Hatchett had seen the contract, he would've told ya, *"Do not sign it!"*

My head was starting to burst. I needed some fresh air so I could think things through. I said, "I'm goin' out for a walk."

My long-time coach and friend went to get his overcoat, saying, "I'm comin' with ya."

Bob and I walked along a street in Manhattan. He had known me long enough to sense when I was beginning to have dark thoughts. He asked, "What's on your mind, Pink?"

I blurted out, "Gonna shoot that guy!"

"Not so loud! People aren't supposed to have guns here in New York."

"Well, I'm packin'." I patted a bulge in the pocket of my overcoat. "It's one of Mr. Smith and Mr Wesson's finest. I wanna see the look on that rat's face when I put holes in 'im."

Bob said, "Pink, do ya remember the night we went to get somethin' to eat and ya told me 'bout all the places ya robbed?"

"Yeah."

"Did ya think God was gonna allow ya to go through life undefeated? Did ya think nobody would ever get ya?"

Bob's words of wisdom hit home. Violence was not the answer. I said, "Bob, you're right. I just gotta deal with it and keep it movin'."

"I'm willing to pay the price.
I'll accept the crumbs right now to get to where I belong.
I know where I'm supposed to be
and I'm willing to work to get there."

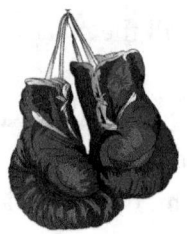

SHARKS BEGIN CIRCLING

I returned to Michigan to celebrate the holidays and shortly after arriving home, received word I had been matched with Jerry Williams at the Miami Beach Convention Center in February, 1980 for a thirty-five-thousand-dollar purse. Jerry was a twenty-nine-year-old black fighter from Fayetteville, North Carolina, six one and two hundred fourteen pounds. He was a staff sergeant in the U.S. Army who compiled an amateur record of one hundred fourteen wins and eleven losses and had been fighting seven years longer than me.

Bob Kaiser and I were booked into the Fontainebleau Hotel along with Fred Corr, Dick Gidron and the rest of their entourage. While in Miami Beach, we stopped in at Chris and Angelo Dundee's Fifth Street Gym, the original training site of my boxing idol Muhammad Ali. Roberto Duran was there getting ready to face Sugar Ray Leonard. By coincidence, Bob Kaiser was a Sugar Ray Leonard lookalike.

Duran was working on a speed bag when we walked in. He stopped, took one look at Bob and rushed him. They were face to face, and Duran was glaring at him. Bob said, *"Mi llamo no es Sugar Ray, mi llamo es Roberto Kaiser."* Duran continued staring at Bob for a full minute. He couldn't believe the man he was scheduled to fight had an exact double.

I didn't help the situation when I chimed in with, "Bobby gonna whup ya."

The Panamanian finally walked away, and Bob said, "He could knock me out, but he'd hafta catch me first, and I can run pretty fast."

I defeated Jerry Williams by a fifth round TKO, but broke the fourth metacarpal bone in my left hand again. Just as I was about to sit down to a late meal, everyone else at my table excused themselves to go to the men's room. It was no coincidence. Dick Gidron wanted to be alone with me. He pulled a roll of cash from his pocket, handed it to me and said, "Here's your money, and I don't wanna hear nothin' else about it, ya hear?" His cold steel eyes challenged me to defy him, but I didn't take the bait.

I replied, "All right, man, I gotcha." I waited until I was alone to count the money. Thirty-five grand had shrunk to twelve hundred dollars. I thought, *Man, I gotta get away from them.*

Meanwhile, Roland Jankelson was not about to let someone steal a project he had put so much time and money into. He took action against me with the state of Washington's boxing commission for breach of contract. The commission ruled in Roland's favor, and I was suspended from any televised fights for four years. If I tried to get a televised fight outside Washington, most other state and local commissions would honor the ruling. The penalty levied on me by the Evergreen State cost me a TV appearance as an undercard to a Michael Dokes heavyweight championship bout and made it virtually impossible to get fights for large purses.

THE SET UP

I told Elbert Hatchett about my problems with Fred Corr, Dick Gidron and the Washington boxing commission. He advised me to go back to Seattle, patch things up with Roland Jankelson and hopefully get my suspension lifted. Fred Corr was infuriated by my walking out on him, but I felt justified after the way he and Gidron had taken advantage of me.

Once I was back in the Pacific Northwest, Roland agreed to let bygones be bygones and arranged things with the boxing commission to have my suspension removed. When we began searching for an opponent, we discovered I had been blackballed by practically all the big promoters. I was having a terrible time getting a fight. Roland finally managed to book a rematch with Jerry Williams on a Bob Arum show at Caesar's Palace televised by ESPN.

We needed a trainer and after seeing the advanced techniques used back east, I realized there was nothing comparable in Seattle. I remembered Bobby McQuiller, who Fred Corr hired to sharpen my defensive skills while preparing to fight Jerry Williams in Miami. Fifty-seven-year-old McQuiller was a five-foot five-inch brown skinned black man originally from Port Huron, Michigan. He fought as an amateur lightweight in Michigan and while serving in the Army during World War II, won national AAU and Golden Gloves titles. Turning pro after the war, he beat future world champ and Hall of Famer Sandy Saddler and appeared on his way to a title shot. His pro career was derailed the following year, 1947, when he whipped Kid Kimitna from South America and The Kid died the morning after the bout. The untimely death of the man he had just beaten soured Bobby on being a prizefighter, and he retired from the ring.

McQuiller relocated to Buffalo, New York and built a reputation as an excellent teacher/trainer. While preparing me to face Williams, Bobby did a great job reviewing films of both me and my opponent and setting up a game plan for the fight. I told Jankelson about how knowledgeable he was and said, "I want to bring Bobby in."

Roland's response was, "Cool." He was all in favor of it.

When McQuiller arrived in Seattle, he insisted, "I'll put you in the best shape you've ever been in, but you'll hafta do everything I say." This excited me and I agreed to his terms. I was shocked after our first workout when Bobby restricted me to two glasses of water instead of my usual pitcher. It seemed strange but whenever I questioned him, he kept saying, "Ya don't need all that water, man. It just slows ya down." He dried me out for six weeks. My reduced intake of water also affected my appetite, making it more and more difficult to eat substantial meals and keep my strength up.

We headed to Las Vegas for the last week of preparation. On the morning of the fight, I had only tea and toast for breakfast, expecting to eat a steak and vegetables around three in the afternoon. McQuiller surprised me by taking me to a metal trailer equipped as a temporary dressing room with a bed, a mirror, a supply of towels and a chair, but no shower or air conditioning. The trailer had been sitting in a hotel parking lot out in the blazing Nevada sun on a day so hot a fire hydrant chased down a dog, chickens laid hardboiled eggs and Satan took time off. Bobby said, "Go to sleep here. You gonna need your rest." He locked me in the stifling hot confines and left me there until eight o'clock at night. When McQuiller came for me, I hadn't had anything except the tea and toast and felt weak. I said, "I gotta eat! I won't have any strength."

He replied, "You're gonna be fine, man, gonna be great."

He sat with me in the trailer until an hour before the fight, when we headed to the regular dressing quarters. Bobby had me skip rope to get loose, and I felt ready to pass out. I jumped rope until a man from the state boxing commission came in and said to Bobby, "He's gonna fight in twenty minutes."

Everything became rush, rush. My trainer brought out half a roll of tape and a half roll of gauze and began wrapping my hands. I said, "Bobby, you're not usin' enough!" His response was simply, "Pink, you're gonna be fine." He pulled my gloves over my thinly wrapped hands, laced them up and taped over the laces. There was no time for any more questions. I had to be in the ring.

Jerry Williams had not been in the greatest shape for our first fight, but was now in superb condition. This was a serious problem confronting me. Another was I had no energy and was so dried out, I couldn't spit.

After the first round, I dragged myself back to my corner and said, "This is crazy! I'm weak. I'm done."

McQuiller replied, "No, Pinky, no, everything's cool."

In the second round, I caught a skull clattering shot and did everything but go down. I was out on my feet, in a daze, staggering all over the ring, when the bell rang to end the round. I went to my corner, sat down and didn't know where I was. I don't remember rounds three through seven. I came out of my mental fog in the eighth round and at the end of the fight, was awarded the decision by the judges. Both hands were broken. I broke the fifth metacarpal bone of my right hand and the fourth metacarpal of my left for the third time and had no idea when the injuries happened.

I later learned Fred Corr paid Bobby McQuiller to make sure I was physically destroyed. Corr was a man who became obsessed with getting revenge on anyone he perceived to have wronged him, no matter how minor the slight. He wanted to make an example of me and end my boxing career. He was disappointed I won the rematch, but pleased I suffered two broken hands and a cut over my left eye requiring seventeen stitches.

I appeared headed for the scrap heap. When I told Elbert Hatchett about what happened, he said, "Pink, you were like a minnow in an ocean full of sharks. It was only a matter of time before they ate you up."

I TURN TO A MARTIAL ARTS MASTER

My flight back to Seattle arrived in time for me to hear a local sportscaster say, "It's been reported Seattle heavyweight challenger Pinklon Thomas will be forced to retire because of his history of teenage drug abuse and brittle bones." I thought, *We'll see about that. I'm undefeated, and not about to give up.* I remembered Muhammad Ali. He had gone to a martial arts master for help with his hands after suffering boxing fractures. I searched for a martial arts studio in Seattle and when I found one, jumped in my 1976 Cadillac Fleetwood and drove there. I had to be very careful driving with casts on both arms and a patch over my left eye. When I arrived, I told the man at the front desk, "I wanna see the master."

He replied, "The master is expected in ten minutes."

I chose to wait and precisely ten minutes later, a short Asian man clad in a gi with long hair down his back walked in. His assistant told him I was waiting to see him. The master walked up to me and said, "I'm John Suk Lee. How may I be of assistance?"

I replied, "I broke both hands in a fight and they say I have brittle bones. Can you help me?" He began pacing the floor and appeared deep in thought. Two minutes went by before he exclaimed, "Yes! I can help you!" I was elated and replied, "Thank you, thank you so much." As I headed out the door, he said, "Eight o'clock tomorrow morning! If you're not here by eight o'clock, don't come back!"

I had never heard of John Suk Lee, but came to find out he was in his late thirties and an eighth-degree black belt. He would go on to train Eddie Murphy for his martial arts fight scenes in both Beverly Hills Cop films.

I showed up at a quarter to eight. John put me in his car, and we drove around. While driving, he outlined the routine we would be following, starting the next day.

John picked me up at my condominium at five thirty in the morning. His headlights were all that illuminated the road as we drove to a section of Seattle with dark, hilly streets. No one was around, and only the sound of crickets could be heard. I felt uncomfortable being in a remote place surrounded by pitch darkness. Stopping at the top of a hill, the martial arts master ordered, "Get out and run!"

I started running, with the master following in his car. If I showed any sign of slowing down along an uphill stretch, he'd honk his horn. This startled me and kept me from slackening off. We continued early morning roadwork sessions for three months, and the results were amazing. I was in tremendous shape, with increased muscle definition and washboard abs. After my stitches were removed, the metal plates taken out of my hands and my hands re-stitched to allow them to heal, the master taught me ways to strengthen my fingers and the tendons in my arms and hands.

While busy working myself into peak fighting condition, two men I met through boxing suffered tragic fates. Jack Stafford, the down to earth soul who played a key role in my development as a fighter, went on a fishing trip and fell victim to nature's wrath. While in the woods near a fishing stream, lightning struck a tree and it fell on him, killing him instantly. Meanwhile, Fred Corr became embroiled in a heated dispute with his sister over their deceased father's house. The place needed numerous repairs and was worth very little, but was where they had been raised. Bob Kaiser kept telling his friend, "Fred, you got a million-dollar home. What are you thinkin' about? Why get so upset about somethin' that ain't worth much?"

"It's the principle, Bobby, it's the principle. Ain't nobody gonna *take* nothin' from me."

Bobby continued trying to persuade his stubborn friend to back off. "My advice is chalk it up to the game and just keep goin'. Let your sister have the headache of that raggedy old place."

Freddie wouldn't listen to his old friend. When Bob told me about the dispute, I thought, *He might try to do his sister the same way he did me. He's a guy who's gotta have things his way, or else.*

A couple of weeks later, Bob called and said, "Freddie Corr's dead. His fourteen-year-old nephew shot him."

The numbers king's unexpected demise was startling news. He had tried to physically ruin me, and it was only through God's Grace I didn't die in the ring during my rematch with Jerry Williams. Corr left an eighty-million-dollar estate, but his wealth couldn't prevent his wrongdoings from catching up with him in an unexpected way. No matter how much a person accumulates, it will never be enough to air condition Hell.

Once my hands healed, I fought California heavyweight Lee Mitchell in Seattle on April sixteenth, 1981. At a minute fifty-three seconds of the first round, Lee drove in to deliver a punch. The instant he made that move, I beat him to it with a punch traveling only a few inches. The blow was given added force because Mitchell was coming in fast toward my gloved fist, and he went down quicker than a plate of Alabama barbeque. It was the type often referred to as a "phantom punch" because it landed a fraction of a second before a camera could pick it up. The punch was similar to the one Muhammad Ali used to knock out Sonny Liston in their controversial rematch. In my case, it was an adaptation of a karate blow John Suk Lee taught me.

The next day, it was announced Lee Mitchell's purse had been tied up because he was suspected of throwing the fight. Everyone in the media claimed they didn't see any punch thrown and if there was no punch, Mitchell must have taken a dive. I was upset with the accusation and thought, "Man, that's crazy! I know I hit him and Lee knows I hit him." The two of us got together and held a press conference at the Red Lion Hotel on Pacific Highway. Arrangements were made to present the fight to the media, using a VCR with slow motion capability.

We showed the fight at regular speed, slow motion and frame by frame. Overly confident barking news hounds watched me hit Mitchell, witnessed his head twist to the side, his eyes roll around, his legs buckle and then saw him fall to the canvas. The undeniable proof punctured their conspiracy theory balloon, and he was able to collect his purse.

After the Lee Mitchell controversy, I was done with Seattle. The state of Washington was the Siberia of boxing and I couldn't get any opponents for big purses, even though I had fifteen wins and no losses. Roland Jankelson had no connections with promoters who could arrange fights for huge amounts. He was a very determined man and I knew in time he would become known by the promoters back east, but I couldn't wait that long. I had to go where the money was, so I could do the best for my family. I decided to head for Joe Frazier's Gym in Philadelphia.

Jankelson was deeply offended by my breaking our contract a second time. When he learned I had gone to Philadelphia, he had the Washington commission regulating boxing contact the Pennsylvania Athletic Commission, and I was prohibited from taking any fights in the Quaker State. I moved my family into southwest Philadelphia. I brought in money by working as a sparring partner for Randall "Tex" Cobb and Smokin' Joe Frazier's sons, Marvis and Rodney.

After five months of going to the gym every day to spar and train, Francis Walker, executive director of the athletic commission, reviewed my case and decided to allow me to fight in Pennsylvania. I fought Curtis Whitner in Philadelphia in November, 1981 and knocked him out in the second round. This broke the ice for me. Shortly after my victory, Bob Lee, the head of New Jersey's boxing commission, decided to permit me to fight in his state. I could now take fights in Atlantic City.

My performance against Whitner attracted interest from Lou Duva, and I signed with his firm, Main Event Promotions. As part of the agreement, I would be trained by George Benton, the man I turned to for advice when Jankelson wanted me to fight Jimmy Young. George, whose skin was the color of black coffee, had fought professionally for twenty one years and was a top middleweight contender in the 1950's and 1960's. His knowledge of boxing was so respected, he was known as "The Professor."

Prior to working with George, I had tried to emulate my boxing idol Muhammad Ali's theory of "Float like a butterfly and sting like a bee. The hand can't hit what the eye can't see." He once dodged twenty-one punches in ten seconds. I would use lateral movement, pull back from punches and dance around the ring to avoid being hit with solid blows. Benton took one look at me and said, "Stop jumpin' around like a rabbit! If you don't bounce, you'll have more leverage to deliver punches with full force. Keep your butt in front of the guy you're fightin'. Work on your defense. Learn how to sidestep, duck, slip punches and block 'em. And keep throwin' your jab. You can knock down a wall with your left hand."

Duva arranged fights for me with Johnny Warr and Luis Acosta. I won an eight-round decision against Warr and scored a second round TKO over Acosta. Lou Duva also matched me with Jerry Williams for a third time at Ice World in Totowa, New Jersey, the most prosperous local boxing club in America. I knocked Jerry out in the second round by connecting with a fluid left, right combination. My record against the Army sergeant was a perfect three wins, no losses.

In the fight game, opportunities can come at any moment, and a pro boxer must be ready at all times. I was scheduled to fight Jeff Shelburg, a Salt Lake City, Utah heavyweight, at the Sands Hotel in Atlantic City when I got a call to fill in for Tim Witherspoon against James "Quick" Tillis in a Saturday afternoon ten rounder from Stouffers Ballroom in Cleveland, Ohio televised by ABC Sports. It was part of a Don King promotion. The entire card was heavyweight bouts and the purse offered was much bigger than what I would be paid to fight Shelburg. It goes without saying I took the fight in Ohio.

Six-foot one-inch Quick Tillis was born in Tulsa, Oklahoma, had eight siblings and entered rodeos when he wasn't boxing. The "Fighting Cowboy's" best event was calf roping. If the heavyweight with hands as fast as a pick pocket won our bout, he would be given a title shot against Larry Holmes, who was going to be at ringside in Cleveland.

The odds were against me because Tillis was ranked third in the world, Angelo Dundee would be in his corner and I had taken the fight on only two days notice. One of the announcers mentioned my fighting on short notice during the telecast, saying, "Pinklon Thomas is the man with the most colorful name in the heavyweight division. He's also the division's 'designated hitter,' responding to panic calls when scheduled fighters don't show up."

As in his previous fights, Tillis looked good in the early rounds but by round four, his tank was empty. The crowd was going crazy, wondering when I was going to knock him out, but I wanted to make him quit. I missed a chance to knock him out in the seventh round and while sitting in my corner awaiting the eighth, George Benton said, "Jump on him. Use the jab and more body shots. He doesn't like it downstairs." I followed his instructions to the letter, and the referee ended the contest by awarding me an eighth round TKO. I was the first to stop the heavyweight known as Quick. His hands were fast, but mine were faster. I should have been allowed to challenge the champion, but that was the last thing Larry Holmes wanted.

With victory secured, I immediately ran to the side of the ring where Holmes was sitting in hopes of witnessing his reaction to my defeating his friend. He had already left. One of the television commentators came up to me and said, "Larry's probably a hundred miles away after watching your performance." My victory over Quick Tillis impressed Angelo Dundee and Don King and proved to everyone in boxing I was a contender.

A brilliant light, color it pink, shone on the dark and dank heavyweight division Saturday night. Pinklon Thomas knocked out Mike Weaver with one beautiful right hand, defended his World Boxing Council title and established himself, if not as the true champion, as clearly the best of what often has been a slovenly collection.

— New York Times

JOINING FORCES WITH DON KING

In 1982, I signed to fight Gerrie Coetzee, a white South African with a "bionic fist," at the Atlantic City Sands Hotel. Nearly five years before, unbeaten twenty-two-year-old Coetzee fractured the second metacarpal bone in his right hand during a fight in South Africa. The hand was so badly smashed it was feared the heavyweight's promising career was over. His physician performed twelve surgeries to remove the smashed joints and cartilage and fuse scraped bones together, welding raw bone to raw bone. The result was a right hand made into a permanent fist that could punch holes in a brick wall.

Coetzee had been given two opportunities to fight for the WBA world heavyweight crown. He lost to John Tate in a bout for the vacant title in 1979, and Gerrie was knocked out by Mike Weaver when he challenged in 1980. By 1982, the South African had worked his way up to the WBA's number one ranking. It was strange that a man who lost both of his world championship fights could achieve number one ranking, but Gerrie Coetzee did it.

Our fight was scheduled for ten rounds and would be televised nationally on CBS Sports Saturday. It was promoted by both Lou Duva and Bob Arum, who hoped to loosen Don King's grip on heavyweight contenders. The WBC would not rank Coetzee because he was from the apartheid state of South Africa, and Arum tried to work around that by having Gerrie establish a residence in New Jersey. I would be facing a South African who was a hometown hero, and had to knock him out if I hoped to win.

The bout was postponed twice, once because of a problem Gerrie had with his right hand and the second time because of a back injury I suffered. After two postponements, CBS Sports put its foot down and insisted the fight take place on Saturday January twenty second, 1983, regardless of anything else happening to either Coetzee or me.

Two days before the fight, I came down with pneumonia. Top trainers advise fighters suffering from colds or pneumonia to start out slow in order to keep from running out of energy in the early rounds. I planned to use the first three or four rounds to feel out Coetzee and see how much I still had in my tank. By the fifth round, the South African had thrown far more punches. When I returned to my corner after that round, George Benton, said, "Man, what the heck are you doin'? You're just standin' around lookin' stupid. Pink, you gotta start throwin' some punches or you're gonna lose this fight. Use a left hook to take away his right hand, then follow with a right."

I followed George's instructions and busted Coetzee good in the eighth round with a left, right combination. Blood gushed from his left eyebrow and continued to flow from the cut in the ninth round. After the ten rounds were over, one judge scored the fight five rounds for the South African, four rounds for me and one tie. The second judge had both of us winning five rounds and the third judge scored it as four rounds for Gerrie, four rounds for me and two ties. It went down in the record books as a "draw by majority decision," and Gerrie Coetzee retained his number one ranking by the slimmest of margins. The result disappointed me, but I moved up to fifth in the rankings.

Two months later, I was scheduled to fight Alfonzo Ratliff in a ten rounder at the Sands Hotel in Atlantic City televised by NBC. It was stopped in the tenth round, and I was awarded a TKO. This put me another step closer to a fight with Larry Holmes to determine who held all the heavyweight titles. He happened to be matched the next night with a Frenchman named Lucien Rodriguez in Scranton, Pennsylvania. Rodriguez had earned the derisive nickname "French Pastry" and was expected to be an easy win for Holmes. While being interviewed after my victory, I was asked by NBC Sports' Marv Albert, "What's next for you, Pink?"

I replied with a big smile, "I want Larry Holmes. I know you're watchin', Larry, and I'm gonna be in Scranton for your fight tomorrow night. You can't miss me. I'll be wearin' a gray suit and pink tie."

While entering the arena in Scranton, I encountered Bobby McQuiller, the backstabber Fred Corr hired to see that I would be injured against Jerry Williams. When he saw me, the short former pro lightweight took off running through the crowd. I chased him, but couldn't catch up before he made it out of the building. I was the last person in the world he wanted to see, so he forgot about attending the fight card.

Thirty-three-year-old Larry Holmes, as tall as me, but with a two and a half inch longer reach, won a twelve-round decision over Lucien Rodriguez. Larry looked sluggish and far too heavy. He had more fat on him than a pig farm and could have filled in for the Goodyear Blimp.

Holmes continued ducking and dodging me. Lou Duva and Main Event were doing their best but without a connection to Don King, my purses were going down from hundreds of thousands to twenty thousand. I wasn't sure where my career was headed when I got a call at home from the bombastic six-foot four-inch promoter with spiked hair. In his sonic booming voice, King bellowed, "PINKLON BABY!"

I replied, "Whazzup?"

Don King said, "I want you to join forces with me. There'll be more opportunity for you, better fights and bigger purses."

"I can't just walk away from Lou Duva. He's put seventy-five grand in me. I can't do that."

"Don't worry about it. He'll get his money back. I'll take care of it. I'll make sure Duva's satisfied."

I said, "Why don't you just give him another twenty-five grand. Give 'im a hundred thousand."

"No problem, man. I'll do it."

I said, "Well, look, gimme a hundred thousand too."

"I'll give ya a hundred grand. We'll do a wire transfer."

I waited an hour to allow King to contact Duva, and then called Lou. He said, "Everything's cool. Good luck. Do what you gotta do." He gave me his blessing.

Within minutes after hanging up with Lou Duva, my phone rang. Don King was on the line again. He made arrangements for me to fly into Pittsburgh and then be chauffeured to his one hundred ninety-four-acre farm near Orwell, Ohio. His half mile long driveway was lined with flags from various countries he had visited in the course of his promotions. In addition to the palatial residence he shared with his charming wife, Henrietta, the grounds also included homes for his son, Carl, and daughter, Deborah, plus a training camp. Every nook and corner of the property was guarded by video surveillance.

I found the irrepressible promoter to be an incredibly intelligent man with a deep sense of human nature. A master at reading a crowd and getting it fired up, Don rose from rock bottom to become a person with the power to change lives.

Needing a training team to keep me in condition year-round, I went to George Benton and asked for his recommendations. He vouched for the loyalty of Willard Barbour and Tommy Hawkins, two dudes from Philadelphia who'd been in the fight game a long time. On George's word, I hired Willard to be my trainer and Tommy to handle physical conditioning.

The first fight Don arranged for me was with Bruce Grandham at the Colise Roberto Clemente in San Juan, Puerto Rico in June, 1984. The promoter who trained his hair to "stand up and ascend to the Heavens" told me, "If you win this fight, Pink, you're in for a title shot." Grandham was a black version of the Incredible Hulk. He walked around like a lumberjack and his hair reminded me of Don King's. In the fifth round, I hit Grandham on the chin like steel driving man John Henry throwing a thirty-pound hammer and knocked him out.

My next opponent would be Tim Witherspoon for the WBC Heavyweight Championship. Witherspoon won the title with a decision over Greg Page after Larry Holmes relinquished the WBC crown because he wouldn't fight Page, the number one contender. I would be the first to challenge Tim for his world title.

Shortly after contracts for the title bout were signed, I was asked to appear at a fundraiser for the Reverend Jesse Jackson's presidential bid. The event was held in Philadelphia's Bellevue Stratford Hotel, and the organizers arranged limousine transportation. Along the way, I struck up a conversation with the driver, a short, stocky black dude built like a tree stump, by asking his name. He replied, "Pete Wiggins."

I asked, "Well, how ya doin', Pete. Are ya from Philly?"

His response was, "Doin' good for myself. Yeah, I'm from north Philly. Say, whazzup, blood. You're Pinklon Thomas, aren't ya?"

"Yeah, gettin' ready to fight for the heavyweight championship of the world.

Gonna be fightin' Tim Witherspoon, your homeboy, in Las Vegas."

"Naw, blood, you're kiddin' me."

"It's for real."

"Dang, man, that's cool."

I asked, "Pete, you do security?"

"Yeah, I do security. I'm a driver and bodyguard for Dr. J and also did security for Pattie LaBelle."

"For real?"

"For real."

"I'm gonna need some security in about a month when I'm fightin' for the title in Vegas. How 'bout if you be my bodyguard that night?"

Pete replied, "Blood, ya know I ain't never been on no airplane."

"Well, you're gonna be on one. Ya can't get ta Vegas 'less you're on a plane."

Pete Wiggins agreed to my offer, so I booked a flight and arranged space for him in the suite assigned to me by the Riviera Hotel. His schedule forced him to take a late flight the night before the championship bout, but he assured me he'd be there to watch my back, see things I might not see and prevent me from being mobbed by fans wanting to get very close and hoping to touch me.

Excitement about my title shot was soon followed by the realization I lacked a manager. Witherspoon was hooked up with Don King's son, Carl King, as his manager and Don as promoter. I needed a manager with ties to the politics of boxing. Angelo Dundee would be ideal.

I called the legendary trainer of Muhammad Ali and maker of many other champions and told him, "Angelo, I've got an opportunity to fight for the world title. Will you be with me?"

"Yeah, Pink, no problem. I'll see you in Vegas in three weeks." He agreed to serve in the unusual capacity of manager, advisor and trainer.

TITLE SHOT
IN THE DESERT

Tim Witherspoon, the man who held the title, was from rough, tough south Philadelphia. He was originally a football player who enrolled at Lincoln University in Jefferson City, Missouri. While catching a pass over the middle, he was speared by a linebacker, and game films revealed it was a late hit. The school never sent him for x-rays. Years later after he started boxing, Tim suffered from back cramps and x-rays showed he had two bent vertebrae because of the linebacker's unsportsmanlike act.

After his football injury, Witherspoon left college, went home to Philadelphia and took a job in the dietary department of a hospital. He gained a great deal of weight from being around food so much and started going to a gym in hopes of working it off. Three months later, Tim entered the Philadelphia Golden Gloves, and that was the start of his boxing career. At one point, Witherspoon worked as a sparring partner for Muhammad Ali, and Ali gave him the name "Terrible Tim" after an extremely rugged gym session. Knowing he was going to be a tough opponent, I trained very hard.

The morning after arriving in Vegas, I did roadwork on a golf course, running with my three sparring partners: Kenny Lakusta, Art Savage and a young kid named Tyrone Armstrong. We spotted thirteen guys running who turned out to be Terrible Tim and his twelve-man entourage. They surrounded us, joined hands to form a human chain and chanted, "KNOCK YOU OUT! KNOCK YOU OUT!"

I glared at Tim and then spun around, pointing a finger at everyone in his entourage. I said, "When I beat you, I'm gonna beat you all at the same time. When you wake up, Tim, ain't nobody gonna be there. Everybody'll be gone."

I broke through the chain and walked away. His taunts made me even more determined to take his crown.

When I told Angelo Dundee about my encounter with Tim Witherspoon, he said, "Pink, there's nothing wrong with wanting to put your opponent on the canvas when you're in the ring, but don't carry a grudge outside the ropes. It doesn't cost anything to be nice and you're better off in the long run to be that way. Being mean and angry makes a person miserable. Why not be happy?" I've never forgotten what Angelo told me. It's a lesson every kid should learn.

I had been training at Johnny Tocco's Ringside Gym on the corner of Main and West Charleston in Las Vegas. The gym had been in operation for over twenty years and was an old school place run by an old school fight guy. Seventy-three-year-old Tocco was originally from St. Louis and had been in the fight game since the age of sixteen. Johnny would be in my corner, serving as my cut man.

Three days before the fight, I was a rock hard two sixteen and warmed up for my last sparring session by punching a speed bag under Tommy Hawkins' supervision. A slim, black retired fighter who had lost his hearing because of busted eardrums suffered in the ring, Tommy was a disciplinarian who said, "Every minute in the gym is unforgiving and ya gotta pour sixty seconds of full effort into each one, baby. Treat 'em like diamonds and gold. Once they're gone, ya can't get 'em back." Tommy kept time during my workouts, toweled me off properly, made sure every item I wore was sanitized and returned to me in plastic bags and saw I was taking in the right amount of water.

My physical conditioner was a man of great energy with a personality that was both engaging and cunning. He wore a hearing aid, but avoided things he didn't want to hear by turning down the volume on the device. There was a stealthy side to him, and he had a talent for digging up useful information by reading lips and through keen powers of observation. He once said, "Gotta keep your circle in a small circumference and protect the perimeter with strong bonds and a coupla delimiters." Not a beat was missed under the watchful eye of "Tommy the Hawk."

I was hitting the speed bag and Tommy, whose hearing issues made him talk in a very loud voice, was timing me to make sure I put in a full three minutes of perfect execution. As the three minutes were about to end, Hawkins was counting down the seconds. "TWENTY SECONDS, BABY! FIFTEEN SECONDS, BABY! FIVE, FOUR, THREE." I hit the bag with a left hook and it burst. It sounded like a bomb exploded.

Tommy said, "I think you're ready, Pink!"

I thought, *First Witherspoon and his entourage try to mob me, now this. What next?*

My bag work finished, I sparred four rounds with rugged looking, curly haired Kenny Lakusta, a Canadian heavyweight from Edmonton, Alberta. He was six one, two hundred pounds and had won all seven of his amateur fights by knockouts. Near the end of the fourth round, Kenny hit me with a left hook and injured my right eye. I suffered double vision in the eye and thought, "Omigod, what am I gonna do?" I decided, "Can't tell anybody, or the fight won't go off."

The night before the long-awaited bout, I was awakened at one thirty in the morning by loud banging on the door to my suite. I heard Pete Wiggins say, "Hey blood, I made it!" and opened the door for him.

Entering the suite, Wiggins dropped his suitcase and asked, "Where's my bed?"

I pointed to the room he'd be sleeping in. Pete entered it, fell across the bed on his back, still fully clothed, and said, "Man, I'm beat from that trip." He immediately drifted into deep slumber with his mouth wide open. Each time he inhaled, a gravelly sound of a jack hammer combined with a wood chipper came from him louder than demons howling from the pits of Hell. I began to worry he might suck the curtains off the windows and the sheets off his bed. After watching my bodyguard built like a fireplug for a couple of minutes, I shook him awake and said, "Man, you're snorin' sooo loud!"

He drowsily replied, "Ohhh, blood, I forgot to tell ya I snore."

I thought, *What have I got myself into?*

There was no escaping the noise of Pete's hard snoring. Even with burying my head in pillows, most of the wee hours went by before I finally dozed off. I ended up with less than two hours sleep. When I awoke, I thought, *I gotta fight Witherspoon with a bad right eye and hardly any sleep. What else can go wrong?*

On fight night, August thirty first, 1984, Jermaine Jackson sang God Bless America. It wasn't the National Anthem, but was pretty cool. Wearing pink trunks and pink boxing boots, I looked over everyone else standing in the ring. I saw Don King swaying and grinning. He was really enjoying the moment. I glanced at referee Richard Steele before making eye contact with my adversary, Tim Witherspoon. I thought, *Tim, my man, I'm gonna put ya to sleep. I'm gonna take ya to school, fool.* Then, I thought about everybody who said I couldn't be a champ; all those who didn't believe in me. I remembered the hurtful words said by my neighbor in Pontiac. "Boy, you ain't nothin' and ain't never gonna be nothin'." I said to myself, "Look at me now. I'm about to fight for the Heavyweight Championship of the World, and I'll do it with a bad right eye if I have to."

The fight began at a slow pace, punctuated by occasional flurries of punches that did more to wake up the crowd than affect the outcome. I kept my left jab in Witherspoon's face all evening, seldom throwing my right. HBO commentator Larry Merchant said, "Witherspoon looks like a rag doll with its head bobbing back and forth." My two hundred seventeen pound opponent mixed up his punches more than me, but never seemed to get into the flow of the bout. I took away Witherspoon's jab, while working mine effectively. By the fifth round, Terrible Tim was discouraged, but all was not well with me. Sitting on the stool in my corner between rounds, I said to Angelo, "I keep seein' two Witherspoon's."

He replied, "Hit the guy in the middle."

I went back out and continued jabbing to Witherspoon's head and body. As the rounds went by, his legs became wobbly, but he never went to the canvas. He was tougher than stainless steel.

When the scheduled twelve rounds were over, Witherspoon raised his hand in victory and I raised mine, but we had to wait for the judges' scoring to be announced. Duane Ford scored the fight 116-112 in my favor. Dalby Shirley had me winning by 115 to 112. Hal Miller called the fight a draw at 114-114. I won by majority decision; and WBC president Jose Sulaiman presented me with a championship belt. It was quite an achievement for a partially blind fighter.

My gross purse was four hundred fifty grand. After all expenses were paid and deductions made, I walked away with one hundred thousand. The money was not the most important consideration. I had a world championship belt and was in the boxing history books; things that could never be taken from me.

"*Don't nobody tell me he don't have no right hand no more.*"

— *Mike Weaver*

A CHAMP UNABLE TO DEFEND HIS CROWN

The WBC held its convention in Montreal during the week following my winning the title, and Michael Spinks, Sugar Ray Leonard and I were scheduled to appear. Pete Wiggins accompanied me to the Canadian city. After experiencing Pete's snoring in Las Vegas, I made sure he had his own room. We decided to go for a walk along the hilly streets.

Continuing to see double, my right eye was getting worse and felt like it was burning. Pete was walking on my left when I said, "Come on along on the right side of me. Raise your hand up, man." I tried to see his hand using peripheral vision, but couldn't do it.

Then I said, "Okay, man, go to the left side and raise your hand up." When he was on my left and raised his hand, I could see it. I said, "Okay, go to the right side again and put your hand up." When he went to the right side, I still couldn't see his hand. I said to Pete, "Somethin's wrong. Can't see outta my right eye."

Once the convention was over, I returned to Philadelphia and went to the Will Eye Clinic. They told me I had a detached retina in my right eye and needed surgery right away. When I asked how long before I could fight again, I was told it would be six months, providing everything went well. A question arose in my mind. "How long could I hold onto my world title without fighting?" I had to call Don King.

When I got the incomparable showman on the line, he was his usual bombastic self. "Hey Pink, baby! What's goin' on, baby?"

It was hard for me to get the words out. I said, "Aw, man, look here. I got a problem. I got a detached retina."

"Aw no, Pink! For real?"

I replied in a very sad tone. "Yeah."

"Which eye?"

"The right one."

"Man, I'm so sorry, man. Look, I guess you're gonna hafta retire, man. You're gonna hafta figure this thing out."

"Don, are you crazy? I just won the championship and you're askin' me to retire? You think I worked so hard to get to this point and then retire? You think I'm gonna quit?"

"Well, what you gonna do, Pink?"

"Ya gotta get me some time. How long can I hold my belt?"

"You can hold your belt for a year."

"Doctors told me it's gonna be five or six months 'fore I can fight again."

"Okay, Pink, we'll see."

After my detached retina surgery, I was bedridden for two weeks. Once I was up and around, I was still under doctor's orders not to run or engage in any exercise. It was a frustrating time of inactivity, and no money was coming in.

My spirits were lifted when my hometown honored me with a three-day celebration in October, 1984. Mayor Wallace Holland presided over renaming the street I grew up on from Fildew Street to Pinklon Thomas Drive. A motorcade with all the latest luxury cars then made its way down Franklin Road to Saginaw Street and the Phoenix Center, where I was honored by Pontiac's councilmen.

The next night, I was the guest of honor at an awards dinner held in the Silver Dome. I was given a key to the city and a lifetime pass to all events held in the indoor arena. Having been the least likely to succeed while growing up, the applause and accolades I received for bringing a championship to the city was overwhelming. I realized my world heavyweight title was the biggest thing to happen in Pontiac. I had done for my city what Joe Louis did for Detroit and Muhammad Ali for Louisville. It made me feel responsible for the fate of my hometown. I considered buying a home in Pontiac until I fell in love with a five-bedroom house in Wyncote, Pennsylvania, a suburb of Philadelphia.

My first title defense was against Mike "Hercules" Weaver at the Riviera in Las Vegas. It was a chance to test my abilities and gain the recognition I desperately needed if I hoped to challenge Larry Holmes in a title unification bout. A native of Gatesville, Texas, six-foot one-inch Weaver had set many of his high school's track and field records and also excelled in football and baseball.

He learned how to box while in the United States Marine Corps, won the WBA heavyweight title from John Tate in March, 1980, but was an inactive champ, fighting only once in twenty-five months. He held the crown until December, 1982, when he lost by technical knockout to Michael Dokes in only sixty-three seconds. Virtually everyone present felt it was a horrible stoppage by referee Joey Curtis, but it came only four months after the tragic Ray "Boom Boom" Mancini versus Duk-Koo Kim bout in which Kim died. Despite losing his crown, Weaver was still regarded as one of the world's most formidable heavyweights and was the number one contender.

I set up training camp in Atlantic City and hired John Suk Lee, the Seattle martial arts master, to assist in my preparation. He watched me like a hawk and assured my sparring, running and eating habits were right where they needed to be.

I left for Vegas three weeks before the fight and was joined there by Angelo Dundee. He was my navigator; a genius at dissecting my opponent's style and coming up with a way for me to counter it. His technical instructions were mainly concerned with which combination of punches I should use and whether I should be stepping right, left, forward or backward to avoid solid hits. With Angelo around, everything became very easy. Going into the fight, I felt free of worries and very positive.

Even though I was sure of my chances, the experts weren't expecting me to pull it off. Oddsmakers made me a slight two to one favorite and HBO commentators Barry Tompkins and Sugar Ray Leonard frequently brought up my recovering from a detached retina.

Angelo astutely pointed out Mike Weaver's habit of carrying his left hand low and dropping the hand after jabbing. I used that information to uncork a five-punch combination in the first round which sent Weaver spinning to the canvas in the center of the ring. He got up before he was counted out. By the seventh round, I could tell he was getting tired. In the eighth, he dropped his hand after a jab, leaving himself open, and I launched an overhand right. It landed along his forehead at the precise instant he was coming toward me and ended the bout. The devastating one punch knockout gave credibility to my claiming to be the true champion of the heavyweight division.

In the post-fight interview, I told HBO's Larry Merchant, "I want Larry Holmes bad. I want him worse'n a monkey wants peanuts." Holmes was at the fight, but avoided me like the plague. He didn't offer any congratulations or shake my hand and told a sports writer, "Pinklon Thomas used his thumb a lot." This was not true. In fact, the unsportsmanlike act of jamming a thumb into an opponent's eye was something Holmes was notorious for.

He also said to the reporter, "Thomas fought a good fight, but wasn't that impressive. Weaver's jab is one of the slowest in the heavyweight division, and he was out-jabbing Thomas." Larry may have been at ringside, but must have had his eyes closed during the fight.

When Holmes' comments were read to me, I responded by saying, "A champion fights everybody. I'm gonna throw some cheese at Larry Holmes 'cuz he's not a man. He's a mouse."

When the man who was ducking me was asked about my response, he said, "If Thomas is gonna buy some cheese, he better throw it to his family."

The boxing community believed Larry Holmes had a stronger claim to the title, but most also felt I was the best heavyweight. The controversy should have been settled in the ring, but Larry didn't want to face me, and I knew why.

He didn't like to be hit with a jab and could only punch fighters who were closing in on his right side. He knew I had one of the best left jabs in the business and would create enormous problems for him. Larry was known throughout the fight community as someone who would agree to the terms of a proposed match, then change the terms by asking for a bigger purse or a higher allowance for training camp expenses. I'm sure he learned his hard-bargaining tactics from his trainer, Richie Giachetti, who was called "No Pockets" because of his "reach impediment." Larry's demands resulted in several proposed fights being canceled, which was fine with him because he preferred holding onto his title by fighting loopholes instead of boxers.

I was gaining recognition as the true heavyweight champion of the world, but my personal life was quickly deteriorating. My wife could not handle the long periods we were apart while I was in training camps, the pressures of the media and family and friends trying to butt into our affairs. I was also feeling stress from covering up my drug abuse.

I had stopped using drugs before turning pro, but knowing boxing and drugs didn't mix and owning a championship belt wasn't enough to keep me from sliding back into addiction. I had become complacent and lowered my guard, instead of being on the lookout for triggers.

Triggers come from unexpected places to cause relapses and lead into downward spirals. An old fighter who had once fought Sugar Ray Robinson and hung out at Joe Frazier's Gym asked me for a lift to his place near Terry Street in Philadelphia. As I drove there, he shared his wisdom about the jab and the best use of a right hand. Arriving at his destination, he asked me in to meet a friend named Sylvia. We rang the doorbell and a dude answered.

From the way he looked outside while opening the door, I knew the place was "busy." It was a dope den. We entered and the old fighter introduced me to Sylvia and two guys named Hank and Grady. She was holding a crack pipe and started to light up. My stomach began rolling as she hit it and then passed it on to the old boxer. I thought, *What in the world have I got myself into?* They passed the "glass barbeque for cooking rocks" to me and trying not to be square, I hit the pipe. From that moment, I was in crack cocaine's death grip and began a secret lifestyle.

My wife and I were no longer one in spirit, could never agree on anything and ended up going our separate ways. Sadly, my son, Pinklon III, was deprived of seeing the house in Wyncote become a happy home. It was wonderfully designed and beautifully furnished, but never more than a place to rest and change clothes. My son turned out well and is presently working as a personal trainer in Chicago.

I couldn't resist the temptations of the night and spent the hours after dark "chasing rocks;" hunting crack cocaine. It made me feel great, especially when I was stressed out. Problems rattling around in my head no longer mattered when I was high. Rather than facing my troubles, I was wasting my life running away from them and seeking shelter in the poison's smoke. My needs had been skewed and thanks to the drug, the fire that burned within me and drove me to a world heavyweight championship was on the verge of fading out. A ghost inside screamed, "PLEASE DON'T LET ME DIE!" but crack deafened me to the pleas of the person I had been.

I never hung around with anyone of celebrity status because I didn't want gossip about my addiction to get into the media. If any "me too fools" in the dope dens recognized me, I would deny my identity, saying, "I'm not the boxer, my name's Tom West." I began avoiding my trainer, Willard Barbour, and not return his phone calls. He came to my house to talk to me, but I wasn't interested in what he had to say because I just wanted to do my own thing. He tried to encourage me to stay focused and keep up my training routine because of upcoming fights. That was not my top priority. Drugs had become the love of my life. With a bunch of money stacked like crisp pancakes, I could get all the dope I wanted. Being a champion did not help me conform to the right way of living and unable to apply the brakes to my behavior, I would be home getting high day in and day out.

Understanding how my system worked and using that knowledge to evade responsibility, I was very cunning and manipulative about my drug use. I never got caught on a urinalysis because I knew all the tricks. If I had a fight coming up, I refrained from doing drugs in order to test clean. After the fight and testing were over, I would go back to the dope houses. Rumors of my being an addict often confronted me, and I denied them every time. I wasn't fooling anyone but myself.

Addicts need to understand that regardless of whom they are, social acceptability does not equal recovery. A socially accepted addict is still an addict. Doctors, lawyers, and corporate men and women who are hooked must face the reality of what true recovery is. To be able to put on an air of success and dignity and continue a secret life is not an advantage, but a serious disadvantage. The only person responsible for an addict's recovery is the addict themselves, and the first steps for them to take are to accept reality and take control of their life and deeds.

Pete Wiggins, who provided my security, was to pick me up one morning and accompany me to a paid appearance. I had been smoking crack cocaine all night and there was still time for me to go to the kitchen for a final hit. I held my glass crack pipe over a gas burner on the stove to heat the residue in the pipe's bowl so it would run down the stem. When the residue was hot enough, I bent over the stove and took a pull on the pipe. I got more than I bargained for because I inhaled not only crack, but gas fumes, and the combination knocked me out. I dropped the glass crack pipe, fell backwards and hit my head on the floor.

When I regained consciousness, Pete was standing over me. He said, "Pink, man, you're gonna lose everything." He picked up the stem that had broken off the pipe.

I got to my feet, approached him and demanded, "Give it to me!"

He replied, "Ya can't go on this way, blood."

Sweat poured down my face like water from a broken tap as I said, "That's for me to decide." The reality was I was losing my choice in the matter.

The man I paid to guard me could only shake his head. I was a lost soul surrounded by insanity and bent on destroying myself. The demonic face of my addiction should have repelled me, but I embraced it even as it grotesquely mocked me.

My second title defense was on March twenty second, 1986 against six foot two, two hundred eighteen and a half pound Trevor Berbick from Jamaica and televised by HBO. Several factors were working against me. Berbick had an inch advantage in reach and legendary trainer Eddie Futch in his corner. Months of drug usage had reduced me to less than fifty percent of my ability. I had also spread myself thin by training and managing fighters and attempting to launch a singing career with a song I had written titled Hanging On To Promises. During the days leading up to the fight, I would be in the casino's lobby selling five-dollar cassettes of my song.

Trevor Berbick and I were the only two ranked heavyweights who hadn't signed management contracts with Don King. After my problems with Roland Jankelson and Fred Corr, I felt more comfortable acting as my own manager. I thought, *I'm the defending champ. Why should I pay somebody a third of my purse to get me fights?* I had forgotten I needed someone to deal with the politics of boxing.

A week before the fight, Berbick signed with Carl King, son of the flamboyant promoter, to act as his manager. Don King called me and said, "Pink, you know what you gotta do. "He didn't have to draw me a picture. It was clear my Jamaican opponent would be the "hometown favorite," and my only chance of winning was to knock him out.

I set up training camp in Los Angeles. Willard Barbour was training me, Tommy Hawkins was my physical conditioner and John Suk Lee was there. John's presence caused Angelo Dundee to decline being in my corner. Angelo insisted on being the loudest voice and didn't feel that was possible with John Suk Lee around.

Hoping I still had a chance to rekindle our relationship for the sake of our son, I tried to contact my wife when I arrived in Vegas, but she was impossible to reach. I hadn't heard from her in eight weeks. She had received twelve thousand dollars from me during that time to cover household bills. A couple of days before the fight, I wired her twelve hundred so she and my son could fly in and be there, but their ringside seats were empty the evening of the fight and they were nowhere to be found.

During the third round, I thought I heard my wife calling my name, but my mind was playing tricks. After the sixth round, I missed Angelo Dundee. He was such a motivator and always made the fight seem easy by reducing what I faced to a simple equation. If my enthusiasm began to fade, Angelo would always say something that would pump me up.

Without Angelo Dundee, I was vulnerable to unexpected treachery. Along with Eddie Futch, Berbick's handlers included Kid Gavilan, a Cuban fighter who once held the world welterweight title, and Lee Black. Black was from the Caribbean Islands and rumored to be a voodoo practitioner.

Lee Black was present in my dressing room to watch my hands being taped, see that my gloves hadn't been tampered with and sign off on a form turned into the Nevada Boxing Commission. Just as my gloves were slipped on my hands and laced up, Berbick's handler used a black marker to draw three stick man figures on the wrist of the left glove. He did it very quickly and went unnoticed. I realized they were voodoo symbols; a form of devil dolls.

He left the dressing room and as he walked out, looked over his shoulder and gave me a gloating smile. I became infuriated at his malignant pleasure and couldn't shake the anger inside me. Angelo Dundee would have calmed me down, but I ended up walking to the ring with a rage filled face. Lee Black had gotten into my head and set me up. I was an angry man lacking the professional mindset required to do what needed to be done, no matter how I felt inside. I had to perform regardless of the circumstances and be ready to take punishment without batting an eye. If Angelo had been there, he would have cooled my rage, but he wasn't and I entered the ring in the wrong frame of mind.

I stormed at my opponent like a bull charging a matador, delivering one hundred sixty punches and connecting on ninety in the first four rounds. I won those rounds, but the white heat of my rage, combined with the toll my drug usage had taken, was draining my energy. After six rounds, I missed Angelo and after nine rounds, I was slowing down. I came back to win the twelfth and final round, and both Berbick and I were arm weary at the end.

Judges scoring the fight awarded seven rounds to my opponent and five to me. If I had won just one more round, the judges would have declared the fight a draw and I would have retained my crown. Ironically, Richard Steele refereed both my victory over Tim Witherspoon and my loss to Trevor Berbick.

It was a major upset because I was a six and a half to one favorite. People I encountered at the airport rudely expressed their disgust with me for losing to the Jamaican heavyweight. One of them brashly said, "Hey, Thomas, you owe me fifty bucks. That's how much I bet on you." I said nothing, trying to avoid causing a scene. I returned to L.A. and every time I stepped out the front door, somebody would tell me how much money they lost betting on me. So many were squawking and growling at me, I avoided people for three weeks.

Feeling frustrated, I wanted to get away from it all. I thought, *I'll go someplace nobody speaks English,* and chose San Juan, Puerto Rico.

One night, I awakened at midnight and was unable to return to sleep. I put on shorts, t-shirt and sandals for a walk on the beach along the same path I did my morning run. After covering a mile, I suddenly turned and looked at the ocean. On impulse, I headed into the water, choosing not to swim but walk. Even when the water climbed past my waist, I kept walking into the abyss. I began to go under, but didn't try to keep from sinking. I felt ready to give up and escape life's harsh reality through suicide.

I suddenly snapped out of it, rose to the surface and began swimming back to shore. Once on land, I began walking, and tears rolled down my face with every stride. I had nearly killed myself because I felt deeply shamed. I was a failure and had let many people down, all because I didn't have the will to prepare for the fight as well as I could have. I asked myself, "Is losing a championship so horrible that I can't go on living?" I looked behind me and saw only one set of footprints in the sand. It reminded me I was the only one responsible for what happened in the ring against Trevor Berbick. I thought, *God is the only one who decides when I leave this world. I live through His Grace and no matter how hard life might become, I still have to live it.* I wanted to pray, but didn't know what words to say. Then I remembered what Momma had said so often. "If ya don't know the right words, just say, 'Thank ya, Jesus. I'm grateful for what's happened, no matter what it is'"

I resumed my training regimen and accepted a ten-round bout in Aguadilla, Puerto Rico against Narciso Maldonado. It had been seven months since my loss to Trevor Berbick. I defeated Maldonado by a fifth round TKO. Soon after that victory,

I received word Bobby McQuiller, who plotted with Fred Corr to end my boxing career, lost his battle with cancer. I can honestly say that, despite what Bobby tried to do to me, it gave me no pleasure to hear of his passing. He was a great trainer who taught me a lot and did a masterful job of preparing me for my first fight with Jerry Williams. It's ironic that the brutal regimen he put me through in Seattle toughened me so that Williams was unable to knock me out in our rematch and I was able to go the distance and win the decision.

In November, 1986, I had a Don King fight in Vegas with William Hosea. I was going through a divorce, and my wife tried to have me served at the weigh-in with legal papers that would tie up my purse. My training team formed a human fence around me to foil the process server and give me a chance to run to my car. Momma often said, "A good run is better than a bad stand."

BATTLING THE BADDEST MAN ON THE PLANET, THEN NEARLY LEAVING THIS EARTH

In March, 1987, I agreed to fight undefeated world heavyweight champion "Iron Mike" Tyson, known as the Baddest Man on the Planet, for the WBC and WBA heavyweight crowns. The fight was arranged by the late Jimmy Jacobs, a world champion four wall handball player who, together with Bill Cayton, managed Mike. Jacobs told me, "Pink, you deserve another title shot." I'll always be grateful to him for providing me with the opportunity.

Don King promoted the bout and when I took the fight, I told Don, "I'm gonna stick and move and beat him. He calls himself the Baddest Man on the Planet, but when it comes to life in general, he ain't as much a man as I am. I forgot more about the game than he probably knows."

Don replied, "I like your confidence."

At that point in his career, Mike was being trained by Kevin Rooney, a disciplinarian he listened to and obeyed. The compact, muscular Tyson had fantastic punching form, particularly on hooks and uppercuts. He had tremendously quick hands for a heavyweight, and this allowed him to land punches in bunches his opponents never saw coming. The punches a fighter never sees coming hurt more than ones they can prepare for or roll with. In addition, Tyson used his entire body correctly, not just his legs, and rarely threw "arm punches." He pivoted with virtually every punch he threw, putting his full weight behind them. This rotation while delivering punches made his hooks and straight rights deadly.

Mike was the most intelligent switch hitter in the history of boxing, making him even more dangerous. He would come at his opponent in an orthodox right handed stance, hit him with a left hook, shift his weight to a southpaw stance, and then nail his opposition with a right hook the guy was falling into. Most of his knockouts were right hooks from a southpaw stance.

Angelo Dundee didn't want me to take the fight, but I insisted, saying, "I can beat him with my jab." I had a three-and-a-half-inch height advantage and a six inch longer reach than Iron Mike and truly believed I matched up well with him. I also said to Angelo, "Many guys Tyson fought were beat before they got in the ring with him. They were afraid they were gonna get seriously hurt. I'm not like them."

When the contracts for the HBO televised fight were signed, Don King held a press conference in New York attended by all the media. Don dressed spectacularly for the occasion, wearing a gold encrusted jacket and waist coat, brown trousers with a crease that could draw blood, a frilled white evening shirt and a fan wing bow tie. His spiked hair quivered with pride.

He grabbed both our hands when he introduced us to the media and said, "Come on, you guys, let's have a stare down! C'mon, Pinklon, look at him."

The man feared for his fists packed with danger was talking some junk, so I extended my left arm, brought my fist to within inches of his face and said, "When I bring my jab back, I'm gonna snatch that gold outta yo' teeth." He responded with a stream of profanity.

In the stories that came out the next day, little mention was made of what was said during the stare down and the focus was on my previous history of drug abuse. The media at that time was sheltering Tyson, and he went into the fight a heavy favorite at six to one. One broadcaster tried to be funny by saying, "Pinklon Thomas oughta sell ad space on the soles of his shoes and make a few bucks while layin' on his back after Tyson decks him."

Eight weeks before the fight, I was in Los Angeles, training under Scrap Iron Johnson at the Hoover Street Gym. Johnson was a black dude from Oklahoma who somehow got to be heavyweight champion of Italy and also fought Smokin' Joe Frazier, losing a decision. I was sparring with six foot one, two hundred twenty-five-pound Mark Will. Mark and I threw right handed punches simultaneously. I hit him on the chest and he hit me where my chest and right shoulder came together. My shoulder popped out, and the pain was excruciating. It brought an abrupt end to our workout.

It wasn't the first time I had problems with my right shoulder. It had popped out while I was sparring with "Laughing Larry" Frazier in Seattle and it happened again while sparring with Marvis Frazier at his dad's gym in Philadelphia. When it popped out in Philadelphia, x-rays revealed it had been broken years before and healed on its own, slightly out of line.

I remembered the original injury. I was in sixth grade and playing in a basketball game. I was a six-foot three-inch center and came down with a rebound against six foot six William Franklin. While attempting to throw a long pass down the court, I cocked my right arm back. William smacked me with his arm and broke my shoulder.

When it popped out in Los Angeles, I went to a Hollywood chiropractor who put me in a sling and gave me an ice pack. He said, "You'll be all right in a couple of days," but he was wrong. Tissues around the joint had become stretched and the shoulder continued to pop out.

Whenever that happened, I would switch over to another part of my training not requiring use of my right shoulder. This was a tremendous hindrance because I wasn't able to skip rope, hit a speed bag or even do pushups. Six weeks before I was to meet Tyson, Angelo Dundee called and said, "Pink, call the fight off, son. It isn't worth it."

My response was, "No, I'm not callin' it off. I'll beat that kid with my left jab." I believed I could beat him because, from the time I was a little boy, I knew I could do anything I put my mind to.

I didn't want to call the fight off because I figured Tyson was knocking everybody out; rapping them on the chin and walking away. I didn't want a great opportunity passing me by. If I didn't fight him then, I wasn't going to get another chance.

I was going into a heavyweight title fight with only one arm. I could hit the heavy bag with both my left and right, but there was no power in my right-hand punches. They had been reduced to little more than taps. My strategy was to outbox Tyson. Mike was used to knocking his opponents out early and fighting very few rounds. If I could withstand a brutal first round and force the fight to go seven rounds or more, I could tire the champ out and go for a knockout.

Three weeks before the fight, I moved my training camp to Vegas and was joined by Angelo Dundee. He served as my advisor and a buffer between me and the politics of boxing. It was critically important to keep my shoulder problem secret. Angelo and I devised a method of signaling with eye contact whenever it popped out.

Leaving his corner to begin the first round, Tyson heard his trainer, Kevin Rooney, shout, *"With bad intentions, baby, with bad intentions!"* Iron Mike came at me like a cyclone and landed a left hook in the first minute that put me into the ropes. Later in the first round, he connected with another big left hand. I suffered a cut on the cheek just below my left eye, and swelling occurred.

In the second, third and fourth rounds, using my experience, I mounted a comeback. I was able to keep Tyson off balance with my left jab, and the judges had me winning those rounds. We spent most of the fifth round in clinches. I was tying him up and pressing my weight on Mike in hopes of tiring him out.

The tactic worked and at the end of that round, Tyson was worn down and almost out of gas. We were in the middle of the ring and I said, "I got some bad intentions for you and I'm gonna get you now," then I turned and headed for my corner.

Before I arrived there, a big fat inspector ran over to me and said, "Thomas, your glove's split!"

I replied, "What you want me to do?"

The inspector shouted, "Angelo, cut it off him!"

I sat on my stool in the corner while Angelo cut my glove off. Spare gloves were required to be kept at ringside for championship fights but on this night, those in charge failed to have them ready. The fight was stopped and someone had to run thirty yards to a supply trailer for a replacement glove. It took time to get through the carnival atmosphere of fourteen thousand fans assembled in a temporary arena set up within the Las Vegas Hilton's parking lot

In the meantime, Tyson was sitting on his stool, arms at his sides, recouping his energy. Thinning haired Kevin Rooney was in his face, shouting, "*With bad intentions, baby! With bad intentions! I want you to breathe, breathe!*"

The delay of nearly ten minutes allowed Mike to catch his breath and revitalize himself. He was refreshed and ready to go. Meanwhile, I had become distraught because of the stoppage and couldn't believe what was happening. As soon as the man returned with the glove, the inspector made things even more stressful when he said, "Hurry up, Angelo," and the bell immediately rang to start the sixth round. My advisor was unable to give me a fight plan for the upcoming round and I was out of my rhythm.

Tyson's plan was to come out and jump all over me. At two minutes of the sixth round, Mike caught me with a sweeping left hook followed by a five-punch firestorm of lefts and rights. My shoulder gave out again and I knew I had no more chance than a chicken in a bag full of cats.

I didn't want to end the fight laid out on the canvas like every other man Tyson had fought. I was able to get up at the count of nine but by then, referee Carlos Padilla had stopped the fight and awarded Tyson a TKO. It was the first time I had ever been knocked down. He won the fight, but I had the satisfaction of standing on my feet at the end.

Mike and I spoke briefly after it was over. I said, "You're a great fighter."

He replied, "You're a great fighter too. I'm the Baddest Man on the Planet, but you're second baddest." Years later, Tyson told sports writers, "My knockout of Pink Thomas was the most vicious of my career."

I returned to my condo in west Los Angeles but instead of resting and allowing my body to recover from the trauma it had endured, I once again let drugs consume me and become my identity. Craving crack cocaine, I drove my white with maroon interior 1986 Mercedes 560SEL into South Central L. A. in pursuit of the poison. I was headed to a gang infested playground for the lawless and taking my life in my hands by having a nine-millimeter handgun and ten thousand in cash in the console of my car. If brains were lard, I didn't have enough to grease a skillet.

Arriving in danger filled Compton, I saw a bunch of menacing cats with tattoos, bandanas and the same color clothes brandishing firearms in broad daylight. They had formed a human barricade to block traffic. The armed thugs were pulling people out of their cars and stealing vehicles one after another. When they came to mine, I said, "Just need some dope."

A dude with an ugly looking scar along his cheek and holding a nine-millimeter asked, "Ain't you the fighter?"

I replied, "Don't know what you talkin' 'bout." He let me drive through because I'm sure he recognized me. A lion can tell a lion, and he knew I was telling the truth about only wanting drugs.

I went to a crack house and lost three days on my 'round the clock diet of crack, cigarettes and liquor. I always went through a lot of cigarettes whenever I did crack cocaine. I ran out of smokes at three in the morning and went for more with an eight ball and a metal crack pipe in my car. Having been up for three straight days, I fell asleep while driving along six-lane Hacienda Boulevard. My car drifted into oncoming traffic, and I woke up to see motorists descending on me with horns blaring. I was too groggy to complete a U-turn and my Mercedes 560SEL sedan coasted into a curb. A man who appeared to be Mexican happened to be walking by. He asked, "You all right? You all right?"

I was unable to say anything in response. He opened the passenger door, grabbed me and pulled me over to that side. He got behind the wheel, straightened my Mercedes out and parked it in a legal space with the windows down. I had a crack pipe, an eight ball, four hundred dollars and a nine-millimeter in the console.

I woke up at six thirty in the morning to birds chirping. Keys were in the ignition, the eight ball of crack was on the floor, my four hundred bucks was still there, my pistol was still in the console and the crack pipe was on the floor. It was amazing. I should have been dead, but wasn't. I honestly believe the man who stopped to help me was sent by the Lord.

During the summer of 1987, my thirteen-year-old daughter PaQuana stayed with me in L.A. Her presence motivated me to cut down on cocaine. We talked about her possibly attending school in California, but she decided not to move in permanently because her family and friends were all back in Pontiac.

PaQuana's mother, Althea, passed away several years ago, but my firstborn and I remain close. She's the spitting image of me, and I have always had a very special feeling for her. She was raised by her mother and four grandparents and turned out to be very ladylike. I am most proud of her. She raised three daughters, has a beautiful home and a successful career as a manager for a company based in Pontiac. Through all my ups and downs, PaQuana has always been loyal to me, and I love her to death.

A MIRACULOUS RECOVERY FROM A STROKE

I didn't fight again until December, 1988, when I was matched with undefeated Evander Holyfield for a $150,000 purse in a ten-rounder at the Atlantic City Convention Center televised by Showtime. I trained in Pontiac, using the basement of a Salvation Army center. James Toney and his manager, a classy blonde lady named Jackie Kallen, were also there preparing for a fight. Known as "The First Lady of Boxing," Jackie was the subject of a feature film titled *Against the Ropes*. She was portrayed by Meg Ryan, and the film was directed by Charles S. Dutton, who also co-starred.

The weather turned unexpectedly cold during my earliest weeks of training, but I still ran each day, with my father following in his car. Sweat would run down into my ears, and the cold numbed both of them and my nose. I didn't think much of it at the time but one day after shadow boxing for six rounds, I leaned on the ropes and slid down to the canvas. Feeling too dizzy to get up, I continued laying there for ten minutes. Jackie Kallen and my father came to me, and I told them, "Lemme lay here awhile."

I finally got up, shadow boxed two more rounds and then collapsed again. This time, I couldn't get back up and had to put my arms around two men's shoulders so they could walk me upstairs. They took me to an emergency room, where I was placed in a wheelchair.

The doctors told me I had an ear infection, but it was more serious than that. My left arm and left leg were useless, my mouth had become distorted, my speech was slurred and my equilibrium was off. I had suffered a stroke.

Not being able to use my left arm or left leg, I had to lie on the floor to sleep. I was unable to sit at a table so when I ate, I had to sit on the floor with my back against the sofa. It appeared hopeless, but I wasn't going to give up. I refused to accept the idea of canceling the upcoming fight.

A week went by and then one day, I took an hour and a half to get dressed, stumbled downstairs and headed out the front door. My father was in the living room with two friends, and they asked, "Where you goin'?'

I said, "Out to run."

They said as one voice, "You can't run in the snow. You'll fall down and there'll be nobody to pick you up. You could freeze to death." I went anyway.

Once outside, I looked at the frost white ground with frozen grass tufts and hard, uneven soil. I was determined to cover a mile. It took me an hour and a half to do it, dragging my left leg all the way.

No one was going to keep me out of the gym. My father understood my mindset and accompanied me there. The first day back, I couldn't throw the left jab I was so proud of and could only paw at the bag. It was discouraging, but I didn't give up. After much struggle and strife, I worked my way back and was rehabilitated, thanks to the Grace of God. My left side has never been a hundred percent since my stroke, but I was able to regain enough use of my left limbs to fight Evander Holyfield, who had been skillfully prepared by George "The Professor" Benton.

Three weeks before the fight, I moved my training camp to Philadelphia, sparring and working out at Joe Frazier's Gym. Right after the World Series, Smokin' Joe mentioned he would be joining in with several other boxers, newscasters, sportscasters, weathermen and other New York City celebrities to participate in a five-mile marathon through Central Park, with the finish line at Tavern on the Green. My trainer, Angelo Dundee, warned me more than once, "Pink, you're gonna need your legs. It's a miracle you've come back this far from your stroke. I don't want you doing any running before this fight."

I should have followed his advice, but my powerful legs and ability to run fast were things I was very proud of. Vanity's fire and destruction got the better of me and I foolishly ran in the marathon. Arriving in New York on the morning of the event, I met Randy Gordon, who at thirty-eight became the youngest man ever appointed to head the New York State Athletic Commission. Randy was one of the entrants and was surprised I would be competing. He asked, "Pink, aren't you in heavy training for a fight?"

"Yeah, man, but I'm in great shape."

"That's good," the commissioner remarked, "but sometimes you can do a little too much."

"Aw, don't worry 'bout it, man. Ya sound like Angelo now."

There is such a thing as overtraining. I was attempting something I wasn't used to doing. Running in Central Park every day was one thing, but training for boxing and suddenly attempting five miles along the park's hilly terrain was expecting too much.

The race took place on a fairly warm day with ideal temperatures for a marathon. I set my usual pace and was among the early leaders. This was not a wise thing to do because, with the uphill and downhill running, I put a strain on muscles different from the ones needed for boxing. The legs I was so proud of were completely shot at the end. I made it to the finish line at Tavern on the Green, but staggered the last forty yards.

My legs didn't come back from the ordeal during the final month of training camp, and I entered the ring a shadow of my former self with no mobility. I faced Evander Holyfield, a punching machine whose blows connected hard, fast and in great numbers. Failing to win a single round, Angelo Dundee had the fight stopped when I could no longer defend myself. I was lucky to last seven rounds against a future heavyweight champ.

It was also my last appearance in a Don King promoted bout. The larger than life boxing personality welcomed me into his home and always treated me with respect. I will be eternally grateful to him for providing me with the opportunity to become a world champion. Don is a man I'm proud to know.

Following the Holyfield fight, my spirit was on life support and I relapsed. An addict never sees the dark side of the moon when they surrender once more to the old pang. I went on a crack cocaine binge, blowing six thousand on the drug in six days. On the last day, my heart felt like it was about to burst. I thought, *If I hit this pipe one more time, I'll be checkin' out for good.* Not wanting the dawn's early light to bring with it my burying day, I put the pipe down. Death was the one thing I feared more than the issues driving me to smoke the poison. I couldn't completely quit the drug, though. The addiction monster still crooned its song in my ear.

MY FINAL FALL

Two months later, in February, 1989, I was standing in front of a crack house at 79th Street and 2nd Avenue in Miami at one in the morning. A cigarette was in my mouth with an ash burned all the way down and about to fall off. I had gone through seven grand chasing drugs the previous week and hadn't slept in seven days. I was pondering whether I should trade my 1987 Pontiac for an ounce of crack. I ended up driving to my condo. The place was a mess. Dishes were piled up in the sink and empty wine bottles were all around. I found a half-filled bottle, chug a lugged the contents and went to sleep.

I slept for thirty-six hours before being awakened by the telephone. It was Angelo Dundee's office manager, Betty. She said, "Get your butt over here. You're supposed to do commentary for a boxing show." I dressed and then drove to Angelo's office. I had lost thirteen pounds and my clothes were much too big on me. Betty said, "Pink, you look terrible."

I replied with hopelessness in my voice and desperation in my eyes, "I can't stop usin' cocaine."

"You need help," was all she said.

Angelo's desk was in the same room with Betty. He listened to our brief conversation, but never looked up from his paperwork. He finally said, "Betty, give Pinklon his files and empty his safe deposit box downstairs."

After I was given the files and the twenty-grand kept in the safe deposit box, Betty walked me out of the building. She gave me a kiss on the cheek and said, "Get some help."

Not knowing what to do, I recalled a prayer my father taught me. *Oh Lord, please give me wisdom, knowledge, understanding, strength and power, and show me the way.* God heard my prayer and gave me the answer.

I went to a bank and rented a safe deposit box. I put eighteen G's in the box and two thousand in my pocket. I went back to my condo, sat down on the couch and cried. My tears flowed because of the terrible things I had done for so many years and the effect they had on those I should have loved most. I had seen my mother age tremendously and suffer from serious health problems, which included diabetes and breast cancer, knowing in my heart that I caused her aging and added to her illnesses. My addiction destroyed my marriage, deprived my son of a happy home and left a stream of agony in its wake. It had cost me dearly and if I didn't become clean and sober I would pay the ultimate price… my life. Too many times, I had chosen what was easier instead of what was right. This time, I would do the right thing.

After shedding all my tears, I got on the phone and started calling treatment centers in Detroit. I didn't want to go through rehab in Miami because I didn't want to embarrass Angelo. I called Sacred Heart and another treatment center, but both were full. I tried the Eastwood Clinics Treatment Center in Royal Oak, Michigan. A lady named Arletta took my call and said there was an opening. I told her my name was Tom West and I wanted to begin treatment as soon as possible. She said, "You can come, Mr. West, but you've got to be clean for seventy-two hours. That means you can start next Monday. You must also be here no later than one thirty in the afternoon."

It was Friday, February ninth. The next day was the tenth, my birthday. I called Arletta in the morning and said, "Today's my birthday. I want to go out and have a drink. I'm not gonna use any drugs."

"I'm sorry, Mr. West. You can't have a birthday drink. You've got to be clean of drugs *and* alcohol for seventy-two hours."

"Arletta, come on now."

"I'm sorry, Mr. West."

"Who else can I talk to?"

"You can talk to Herb, but he's not in yet. Call back in an hour."

I called back an hour later and was connected to Herb. I was surprised to hear a delicate feminine voice answer, "Hello?"

I said, "Hi Herb, I'm Tom West."

"Mr. West, what can I do for you?"

I couldn't get over how womanly the male drug counselor's voice was. "Herb, I talked to Arletta. She told me I can't have a drink on my birthday, which is today. It's my birthday, man. I want to celebrate with just one drink. I'm not gonna use any drugs."

"Oooh, I'm sorry, Mr. West, you can't do that."

"C'mon, man."

His voice took on the tone of a scolding female school teacher. "Hey, forget the dumb stuff! Look, Mr. West, you come here and we find your system isn't clean, you can't get in the program." He hung up on me.

I was infuriated and thought, *I'm gonna really put somethin' on that chump when I meet up with him.*

Most other residents in my condominium development were senior citizens, and I had made friends with Ellie, an older Italian woman with salt and pepper gray hair and ruddy cheeks who lived on the other side of my unit. We had gotten to know each other because she would walk the complex when I would be running.

I told Ellie about my plan to enter a treatment center in Michigan, and she was all for it. She said, "Pink, do it the way they want. We'll celebrate your birthday tonight, and you'll have a good time without having to drink."

We went to Tony Roma's Steakhouse in Doral, Florida and the only beverages I had were grenadine and Perrier water. We toasted my birthday, and I stayed clean.

My flight to Michigan would be leaving early Monday. Late Sunday morning, I knocked on Ellie's door. When she answered, I told her, "I gotta go back over to the dope house."

"What are you talking about, Pink?"

"Ellie, I gotta pay the dope man."

"No, Pink, you're not taking me there."

"Ellie, please, I gotta go. Gotta pay the dope man." Paying the drug dealer what I owed meant a great deal to me. I always believed in paying my debts, whether it was to a drug dealer, car dealer or any other kind of dealer. I didn't want the debt hanging over my head and revolving onto me some way. The look in my eyes told her I was determined to get the money to the poison peddler. Ellie realized if she didn't go with me, I'd never come back and never get clean.

She took a deep breath, exhaled, then said, "Pink, I'm gonna drive you, but I'm gonna leave the engine running and if you're not out in thirty seconds, I'm taking off and leaving you there." The resolve in her eyes told me she meant every word.

We arrived at the dope den and I opened the passenger door. Just before I got out, she said, "Remember, if you're not out in thirty seconds, I'm leaving you here."

"Ellie, I'll be out. Just don't leave."

I jumped out of her car, ran to the door of the house and knocked. A guy I didn't recognize answered. I asked, "Where's the man in charge?"

"In the back," he replied.

He led me toward the rear of the place. There were others in the wretched hive of self-destruction and I recognized some of them. They knew me as Tom West. I had sometimes treated them to crack, and they hoped I was feeling generous. They greeted me, saying, "Mr. West, Mr. West! Whazzup, Mr. West?"

With no time to waste, I went into a bathroom, closed the door behind me, put my left foot on the toilet, reached into my sock and pulled out eight one hundred-dollar bills. I opened the bathroom door to find the man who ran the crack house standing there. I showed him the money and counted it out into his hand. He had an astonished look and said, "What's happenin', Mr. West? What's goin' on?"

"I'm gettin' outta here. I'm done."

"Man, what you talkin' 'bout?"

"I'm done. Gotta get outta here. I gotta go. See ya later." I was worried my thirty seconds were used up and Ellie had left. If that were true, I'd be doomed and end up dying a junkie.

I ran to the front door, opened it and split without taking time to close it behind me. I sprinted to Ellie's car, jumped in and she took off with tires smoking. We were both perspiring hard; me from stress and physical exertion and her from the tension of waiting to see if I'd relapse or not. When we returned to her place, she cooked me a nice Italian meal and then I went to my unit and turned in early.

The next morning, she drove me to the airport and walked me to the plane. She didn't leave until I had boarded, the door to the cabin was closed, boarding stairs were wheeled away, my plane taxied down the runway and it lifted into the air. If not for Ellie, I would be dead today.

"I've had to deal with so much in my life.
Anything that comes up now is a secondary problem.
I don't let it bother me."

CLEAN AND SOBER

It was already twelve thirty in the afternoon by the time I claimed my two suitcases and hired a cab. If I wasn't at the treatment center in an hour, I wouldn't be accepted. In my haste, I had forgotten to write down the center's address. The driver thought he knew where the place was, but it turned out he really didn't. I had to stop and use a pay phone to call for directions. My forehead wrinkled as I worried about cutting things too close and being turned away after traveling so far.

We arrived with a minute to spare. The sun was out, but bitter cold turned my breath to smoke as I raced to the front entrance and then up a flight of stairs to the office, carrying a heavy suitcase in each hand.

Entering the intake department, I announced in a voice hoarse from the cold, "I'm Tom West. I'm here to see Arletta."

A golden skinned black woman with an Afro said, "I'm Arletta. Have a seat Mr. West. We've been expecting you."

I felt like saying, "Ya tell me, 'One thirty or else,' now ya make me wait!" but kept my mouth shut. I thought, *Pink, you're gonna hafta do things their way, 'cuz your way didn't work.*

I waited ten minutes before Arletta had me sit across from her at a desk. She began by saying, "I'm glad you made it here. You're in the right place. You're not alone, and things are going to work out." She asked for my insurance information, and I told her I would pay in cash. A month at the treatment facility cost six thousand dollars. I counted out the bills and when finished asked, "Can you hold some money for me?"

"Of course, Mr. West."

I counted out three thousand, giving Arletta all I had left. She wrote a receipt and placed the money in a locked metal box, saying, "I'm the only one with a key to that box. Anything else I can do for you?"

"Yes," I replied, "I wanna meet Herb."

Arletta picked up her phone, dialed an extension and said to the voice on the other end of the line, "Jerline? This is Arletta. Can you come to intake? Someone wants to meet Herb." After hanging up, she said, "Jerline will take you to him."

Within five minutes, a chunky, light skinned black woman wearing glasses came through a door marked "Authorized Personnel Only." Arletta introduced me, saying, "Jerline, this is Tom West. Please take him to Herb."

Jerline led me to a room where a stocky, flamboyantly dressed black man with a Jheri curl and a diamond studded earring was sitting at a desk. She said, "Herb, this is Tom West. He wants to talk to you."

We stared at each other until Jerline left us, simultaneously having a moment when a million words were spoken without talking. Herb broke the silence by saying, "Tom West, my foot!"

We had immediately recognized each other. Herb had grown up in Pontiac and was part of a group of gay addicts I often saw in the dope dens. We were using the same drugs, buying them from the same dealers. The last time I saw him, he was balled up in a corner of a Laundromat. He had transformed into a man of high fashion with a good job. Realizing who he was, I was no longer angry about how he treated me on the phone.

I said, "I been a lotta places and done a lotta things. I became heavyweight champion of the world, but I can't stop smokin' that dope." I began to weep.

Herb responded in a gentle, soothing voice. "We ate the same dirt and had some of the same demons. Shoulda seen me when I first came here. I was a mess and didn't know from nothin'. All I ask of ya is stay here and work the program."

"By the way," he added, "want me to put your name out to the others and let 'em know you're Pinklon Thomas, or ya wanna say you're Tom West."

"Tell 'em I'm Tom West."

He nodded his head and replied in his delicate voice, "Okay."

When group sessions began the next morning, I introduced myself by saying, "My name's Tom West, and I'm an addict." Once the introductions were over, Herb made it clear the center was not a place to rest, saying in his stern female schoolteacher voice, "This is not prison or jail. This is not the real world. This is *your* place to work hard finding *yourself*." Without access to phones, the treatment center had become our world and our journeys to self-discovery would be free of distractions.

It was a wakeup call for me. I had to get busy uncovering and discovering the exact nature of my nature. Sobriety was much more than putting down my crack pipe. I had to face the deep-seated issues driving me to the poison.

Any hope of getting away from the world of secrets, lies, deception and betrayal I had created required being totally honest with myself and those around me. The first task was revealing my true identity to the other patients; a huge step requiring total commitment to the program. I had been there four days when I overhead two patients talking. One said, "Ya know that dude Tom West? Well, that ain't his real name. He's a fighter. Can't remember his name, but I know he's a fighter."

The next night, Dexter, one of my three roommates, came to me. He was in his forties, five ten, beer bellied, so light skinned he was darn near white and without a tooth in his head of his own. With a knowing grin, he said, "Ah know who you are. You Pinklon Thomas."

I replied with mock outrage, "Man, I don't know who Pinklon Thomas is and don't know what you talkin' 'bout."

I lay awake that night and decided I had to get real. Secrets I'd been holding and burying deep inside were the roots of my garden of despair. I had to be honest with myself and the others in the program if I hoped to recover from the disease of addiction.

When it came time for me to share in the next day's first group session, I announced, "You've been told my name is Tom West, but it's really Pinklon Thomas. I'm a former heavyweight champion of the world."

Dexter shouted, *"Ah knew it! Ah knew it! Ah knew who he was!"*

I replied, "Man, I'm just like you. I'm here tryin' to get well."

I worked the program the way I was told and accepted their way of doing things. I was taught a very important lesson about triggers that could suck me back into the druggie way of life. After my second week, I was clean, felt great and was ready to go home. I went to Arletta and said, "I'm gettin' outta here. I gotta go."

"Where you gonna go?"

"Goin' back to Miami."

"What are you gonna do there?"

I replied with a wide smile, "Don't know. Might try bein' a country western singer, but I gotta get outta here. I'm clean. I feel great."

"Tell you what," Arletta said. "Herb's off today. Stay here 'til he comes back.

I'll have him talk to ya first thing when he gets in."

Next day, I got up, had breakfast and then went to see Herb. I announced, "I'm gettin' outta here."

"What you mean you gettin' outta here?"

"Herb, I'm gone. Gotta get outta here. I'm all right. I'm clean."

He responded in a voice which sounded like a mother talking to her son. "Pink, lemme tell ya what's gonna happen. You're gonna get in a cab and tell the driver to head for the airport but along the way, you're gonna cop some dope on Eight Mile Road and end up in a hotel room or dope house. You're gonna relapse and get right back to the drugs."

I said, "Naw, Herb, I ain't goin' out like that."

"Pink, I'm tellin' ya what's gonna happen. Tell ya what, if ya wanna go, ya can go. But do me a favor." He handed me a cassette tape and said, "I want ya to listen to this."

I said, "Okay," went up to my room and inserted the cassette into my tape player. I looked out the window while listening. It was sunny, but snowing, and so cold, frost had formed on the window. The first songs were by James Cleveland, a Chicago born singer known as the King of Gospel Music. In a deep, powerful voice that could shake thunder from the skies, he sang, "Nobody told me the road would be easy, but there's something about walkin' with Jesus. I don't believe he'd bring me this far just to leave me."

The words struck a chord within me and a thought flashed in my mind, "It's up to God if I recover. Gotta put myself in His hands. He won't abandon me if I stay here, but I'll be turnin' my back on him if I leave. If I do that, I'm doomed."

Patti LaBelle followed Pastor Cleveland's songs. She sang, "I'm tired of you puttin' yourself down. In spite of all you've been through, I still believe there's a winner in you." The music touched me at my core with a powerful emotional impact. It sent the message, "It's a serious mess you got yourself in, but don't get me wrong. You'll get through this because I know you're strong."

Her words moved me so, I began crying, couldn't stop and began to worry I'd flood the room with my tears. After listening to all the songs and crying until I could cry no more, I took the tape back to Herb and said, "Okay, I'm not goin' anywhere." The man with the sweet feminine voice put an arm around my shoulder, pulled me into a side hug and said, "Thank you, Pink. Couldn't bear to see you relapse. Ooh, it hurts so bad deep inside whenever one of my patients goes back to drugs."

I replied, "Thank you, Herb, for all you've done" and went back to my room. More than anything, I wanted to recover. I spent the rest of that day in my room working on the Fourth of the Twelve Steps, the "Inventory Step" — writing out the story of the family and friends I hurt through my self-destructive behavior. I intended to apologize to each and every one of them.

Our routine included being loaded onto a bus and driven to Narcotics Anonymous meetings in nearby towns. Everyone at the meetings treated each other like family. We were brothers and sisters and though no one completely liked everybody, we helped each other by showing empathy. We deeply knew how bad things can get because of dope and the horrible effect chemicals can have on a human body. While hating the persons we once were, we also realized each of us had battled a powerful force and needed mutual support to stay clean and continue lifelong recovery. Sharing our experiences by getting up and telling our stories was part of the process.

Like everyone there, I would stand up and introduce myself. "Hi, I'm Pinklon and I'm an addict." Addicts tend to live drama filled lives, and the NA meetings were better than a movie, plus the coffee was free. I was drinking more coffee than ever before. Herb assured me in his soft, feminine voice there was nothing wrong with that. "Addicts need stimulants to replace their dope. Some smoke, some eat candy and others become coffee drinkers."

As the weeks went by, I began to understand that since I was the one who had seriously wrecked everything, I was also the one who could make the changes to salvage my life. For the first time, I realized I had within me what it took to turn things around and change for the better. This empowering thought was a breakthrough. I was ready to go out into the world free from any cravings that tied me down and caused me to behave irrationally. With my new-found self-knowledge, I would become an oncoming storm and make my sobriety a force to be admired and to inspire.

On my last day at the center, I said goodbye to Herb and thanked him for all he had done. I said, "It's hard keepin' it together through stormy weather that rarely gets better but step by step, I'll keep movin."

"Stick to the script," he replied in his soft voice. "It'll get ya through to the light at the end. If ya do that, that's all the thanks I'd ever want."

The Eastwood Clinics Treatment Center was sixteen miles from my parents' home, but only Ellie knew where I was. I went to my mother and father after leaving the center. They were pleasantly surprised at my unexpected arrival and welcomed me with open arms. After I told them about my addiction and my stay at the treatment center, they assured me of their support, as long as I stayed clean.

After five days of visiting, I received a call from Betty, Angelo Dundee's office manager. She said, "Angelo would like you to appear with him and other champions on a TV show called Secrets of Boxing that will be done in Orlando within a few weeks." I couldn't believe Angelo knew where to find me. Elated at being included in the production, I gladly accepted the opportunity and immediately headed back to Florida.

I returned to Miami a patient man, truthful about himself, who found contentment in such simple pleasures as the sight of a sparkling, splashing fountain in the morning sunlight. I said to myself, "I can stand up now with a smile or frown 'cuz I know I won't be knocked back down by that poison. No matter where I sit or where I stay, it'll never be dark and never be gray. It'll be wonderful and colorful, like a bright sunny day."

It happened to be Wednesday when I walked into Angelo Dundee's office.

He asked, "How's it going, Pink?"

I replied, "Best Wednesday of my life, and each day tops the last one."

Angelo was amazed at the change, telling me, "You're the greatest." When he said that, I replied, "You don't mean that. How can I be greater than Muhammad Ali?"

His response was, "I'm not talking about what you did in the ring, but how you got away from the drugs and lifestyle that had you on track to losing everything, including your days on this earth. You went through more stuff than Carter's got pills and showed amazing heart, soul and spirit. When you realized what drugs were doing to you, you proved yourself a champion and came through with flying colors. Pink, you can accomplish any goal you choose for yourself."

I could never thank Angelo enough for all he taught me, especially his favorite saying, "It doesn't cost anything to be nice." He always welcomed people with a smile and a gracious hello. Angelo was a "human Hallmark card" who could cheer up anyone. He trained fifteen world champions, but never showed the slightest sign of arrogance or aloofness. Both Angelo and I were among the first class of inductees to the Florida Boxing Hall of Fame in 2009. I felt deeply honored to be placed in such elite company. Having known Butch and Kathy Flansberg, the backbone of the FBHOF, since the 1990's, I treasure their friendship.

Angelo, the legendary trainer, never forgot me and we remained close friends up to his passing in 2012. His death left me speechless. I couldn't stop crying, but had to let it out.

He was the man who introduced me to my boxing idol, Muhammad Ali. We first met at the Fifth Street Gym in Miami soon after Ali began to show symptons of Parkinson's Disease. We became friends and during his later years, I once told him, "You have security, but remember I'm your bodyguard. I'm ready to take a bullet for you."

The boxing legend replied, "I'm glad you're with me and watchin' my back. The way you came back from all your problems shows me you can handle anything."

Muhammad Ali was the greatest because he gave a flavor and texture to his era and stood for important things outside the ring, such as courage, pride, dignity and the brotherhood of mankind. I'll never forget the time I saw him on the evening news talking a man bent on suicide off a ledge in Los Angeles. Ali told the distraught man, "I'm your brother." He spoke from the heart, said what he truly felt and in so doing, saved a life.

Muhammad Ali was nothing more or less than a great human being who spent the last half of his time on this earth building bridges to bring people together. I was in Louisville, along with other boxing champions inspired by The Greatest, to pay my respects when he passed away in June, 2016. To a man, our sentiments were, "May God make The Greatest the Purest."

I detested what Larry Holmes did to Ali when they fought in 1980. He violated all rules of sportsmanship. Muhammad had been weakened by thyroid medication taken to lose weight, and it left him drained of energy for the fight. In addition, Larry had old time trainers who taught him nasty tricks, like sticking a thumb in an opponent's eye. Holmes inflicted an unnecessarily vicious beating before the fight was stopped in the eleventh round. The actor Sylvester Stallone, who was sitting at ringside, said, "It was like watching an autopsy on a man who was still alive." It was later reported that what Holmes did contributed to Ali's Parkinson's issues. I vowed if I ever got in the ring with Larry Holmes, I'd do a number on him. I believe he knew this and did all he could to see it would never happen.

...A smile that could light up the world and make a person

forget everything else..."

THE PRIZEFIGHTER
AND THE LADY

After finding a better way to live and no longer desiring drugs or alcohol, I felt it best to start off fresh in a new city. I wanted to avoid setting myself up for failure by becoming involved with people, places and things that could trigger a relapse. Michigan, Miami and Philadelphia were out.

I was contacted by a fight promoter named Dick Fleming, who had been associated with George Foreman. Dick was a well-established roofing contractor based in Orlando, Florida with a passion for boxing. He was very supportive and proved to be a trustworthy person. I found it interesting that he was born February eighth, while my birthday is February tenth.

We came to an agreement which gave me a monthly stipend and use of a small three hundred square foot one-bedroom apartment. The Howard Johnson on Colonial Drive in downtown Orlando agreed to provide my training facilities. Dick also arranged for a chiropractor and fight fan named Tom Teleky, who we called "Doc," to serve as my cut man. In addition, my manager negotiated a sponsorship deal with a Hertz Rent A Car agency that gave me use of a different brand-new car each week.

October tenth, 1989 marked my eighth month of sobriety. I had taken my first step toward recovery from addiction, but realized I had only just begun the journey to becoming a compassionate man of honor and dignity. A confused human being with demon allure had lived inside me for too long and kept me from achieving my structure and potential. I had failed so many times at measuring up to my parents' high standards and wondered if the Lord would allow me another chance at becoming a good person. Thankfully, an opportunity presented itself, but in an unexpected way.

It was the week after Thanksgiving in 1989 and I was working out in a gym on Orange Avenue in Orlando. I noticed a beautiful woman with a unique exotic look. I thought she might have been black, but wasn't sure. I had never seen a black woman with long straight hair all the way down her back, a widow's peak and blue eyes. I went over to her and said, "My name's Pink. What's yours?"

She responded with a smile that could light up the world and make a person forget everything else. "My name's DaJuana, but those who know me call me DJ."

I asked, "Do you eat soul food?"

"I not only eat it, I cook it."

She was probably black, but there was the question of her blue eyes. I said, "I've never met a black woman with blue eyes before."

She gave me a quick smile that showed her white, even teeth, and then replied, "Oh, they're contact lenses."

I asked if she came to the gym often and she said, "Oh yeah, I do martial arts."

I asked her out to dinner and she accepted. During the meal, DJ told me she had been recently divorced and was holding down two jobs, plus doing modeling and acting part time. I asked, "Does your ex help out much?"

She bit her lip and her eyes searched my face before she said, "Oh no! I'm afraid to ask him for anything. I'm scared to death of him." I could see my question caused her a moment of emotional pain. She lowered her eyes and said in a quieter tone, "He beat me up bad."

"A real tough guy, huh?" I replied. "Any man who hits a woman is a coward."

"Oh, he's tough. He's a power lifting bodybuilder who can bench three hundred pounds. He showed off once by lifting the back end of a car. He also used cocaine, and probably still does." She added, "I can't stand anyone involved with drugs." The look in her eyes told me she meant business. I had a bad feeling she might not want anything to do with a man in recovery.

She didn't mention anything about my being a heavyweight champion. I thought, *Maybe she doesn't know I'm a fighter.* Since the media always mentioned my history of drug problems, I decided not to bring up my boxing career. I had been sober nine months, but was reluctant to chance frightening her away with my past.

Her two full time jobs were working for Orange County as a teacher's aide for special needs children from seven until three in the afternoon and as a juvenile detention officer for the state of Florida from three thirty in the afternoon to eleven at night. DJ was off from both jobs the next day and invited me over to her apartment.

It was spotlessly clean and lavishly furnished. When I walked in, I was surprised to find her wearing several sweaters and two pairs of slacks. She offered me something to drink, and I had water while she had a wine cooler. We sat across from each other while she talked about her life.

She took a sip of wine, before saying, "My ex is a vicious, frightening man." She took another sip, then added, "It's very difficult for me to trust men after what I've been through."

The more we talked, the more we realized how much we had in common. She had grown up in Flint, Michigan, only forty minutes from Pontiac. Whenever

DJ took a modeling or acting assignment, she coincidentally used the last name "Thomas."

She also told me she was adopted. Her father had served in the military, retired from General Motors and had done very well in real estate. Her parents owned homes in Michigan and Orlando, and she had grown up accustomed to the finer things in life.

We didn't plan it that way, but saw each other every day for two straight weeks. I was worried about her, and she just had to see me. After the two weeks went by, I became very concerned that the beautiful aspiring model/actress with hands of a princess and features of an angel wouldn't accept me as the man I had become. I couldn't keep the truth from her any longer, so I told her, "I'm in recovery from alcohol abuse and drug addiction. I've been sober ten months." It was a relief to find her very understanding. She said, "I'm glad you're putting your life back together. I hope you keep it up."

I replied, "I've placed my life in God's hands, and that's how I've stayed sober."

"Good," she said."I can see a peaceful quality about you. It gives you a presence."

We began learning more about each other. DJ asked me to go with her when she consulted a clairvoyant named Miss Katie. I didn't believe in fortune tellers, clairvoyants, or people like Mrs. Malloy, who had the rooming house in South Carolina, but I went with her. Miss Katie told us, "You're in love with him, but he is not in love with you. As time goes on, he's going to be deeply in love with you." Hearing that, I rolled my eyes because I'd never been deeply in love with anybody. I was very fond of DJ, but that's as far as it went. I thought, *All those years actin' like a gangster and usin' drugs, I forgot how to love, or maybe never learned how.*

I also accompanied D.J on a visit to her ex-husband and his parents. While there, her former spouse disrespected her. He probably was trying to goad me into a fight, but I spoke to him in a calm, yet firm, voice. "You will not disrespect DaJuana whether you're in my presence or not. I don't care about your daddy sittin' here or your momma over there, but I'm lettin' you know you will not disrespect her... *ever.*"

Knowing I meant what I said, he did a one-eighty. I looked him dead in the eyes, while sitting on a couch with my arm around DJ and conversing as though I hadn't said anything to provoke him. The thick muscled bully was quiet as a mouse for the rest of the visit.

While driving home, DJ said, "Pink, baby, my ex was used to runnin' off all my boyfriends. When he said that nasty thing to me, I thought, omigod, he's gonna kill Pink right here and now."

"No, he wasn't," I replied. "No one was gonna die tonight unless I did the killin'."

DJ didn't know I gave out butt kickings for a living.

She said, "Honey, I was sweatin' bullets until you talked to him in that calm, strong voice and gave him that intense look with your steely hazel eyes. It was the first time I encountered the power within you. I'll never be afraid of that man again."

I had admitted I was in recovery, but was still reluctant to reveal my entire past to DJ Fearing she might not accept me with all the skeletons in my closet, I then realized how the consequences of reckless behavior were making it extremely difficult to be completely open with a woman I was becoming romantically involved with.

When she saw my tiny apartment, it helped my charade of keeping part of my life secret. However, the fancy cars I was driving, thanks to my sponsorship deal with the rent a car agency, gave DJ concern. She asked, "How can you afford those cars? Be honest with me. Are you dealing drugs? If you are, I want no part of it and it's over between us."

I told her I was doing promotional work for Orlando's Church Street Station, a venue for dining and entertainment attracting many tourists. We sometimes met there and several people in management knew me, so she bought the story.

In the beginning of our relationship, I showed her only my polished side. I was always on my best behavior and tried to be the perfect gentleman. The more I talked to her, the more she told me what she would and would not tolerate, and I gained a sense of when to bring up certain topics. I also began to understand all the obstacles going through her mind and did all I could to assure her she wouldn't have to worry about them. I said, "I'll be there to run interference for you."

I began romancing the woman who fascinated me by showing up with delicious meals for her dinner break at the juvenile detention center, always including a rose with the food. She became accustomed to it, but reminded me she was on a schedule and had to eat at a certain time. She said in jest, "My food better be here on time, or else." She still didn't know anything about my fight career, but some of her male co-workers kept saying, "Your boyfriend looks very familiar." I was able to keep up the deception because information was harder to come by during those pre-Internet times, plus I hadn't had any fights since moving to Orlando.

As part of my campaign to win her heart, I serenaded her with love ballads every night. I would sing in her apartment or while driving around. She'd say, "You have the most amazing voice ever."

I'd reply, "It's easy with the inspiration you give me."

I learned even more about the woman who was moving deeper into my heart with each passing day, when an important matter required an urgent last-minute trip to Miami. I only had three hours to get there. I told DJ about it and said, "I don't know what to do."

She said, "I can get you there in time."

"Miami's four hours away."

"Don't worry, Pink, I'm the best driver you've ever seen."

We left immediately and were blasting along the Bee Line Expressway with the speedometer needle hovering near one hundred. She was in complete control and totally relaxed as if on a Sunday afternoon drive.

As we approached the exit we needed to get off at, she said, "Gotta pay a toll. Pink, reach into my purse for the money."

We flashed by the exit and I exclaimed, "You went past it!"

"Don't worry, Pink, I'll get back there. Just see if I have the money." Lucky for her, there were no other cars around. She moved over to the furthest right lane, stopped the car, put it in reverse and blasted toward our exit at high speed. She did it so smoothly I wasn't at all nervous. I thought, *This lady can really handle herself.*

While fishing through her purse, I found a snub nose .38. I pulled it out and asked, "What's this?"

"Oh darn, you weren't supposed to see that. That's to protect your big butt.

I don't want my ex tryin' to run you off and ruin our good thing."

I began twirling the revolver on my finger and said, "Ain't that cute." I had found a woman who would watch my back and became swaddled in my love for her.

Deep thoughts distracted me, and I forgot we were coming up to a toll booth.

DJ said, "Put it away. Who do you think we are, Bonnie and Clyde?"

We made it to Miami in two hours and forty-five minutes. Thanks to DJ's skill behind the wheel, I was able to handle my business. We returned to Orlando at a leisurely pace, and I sang hits by The Originals to her all along the way. My feelings for the one in a million lady had graduated from friendship to a love so strong, I couldn't imagine anyone else ever feeling that way.

The holidays were approaching and DJ gave me a Christmas present: A key to her apartment. She entrusted me with the key so I could get in if she hadn't arrived home from work, and I knew violating her trust in any way would remove me from her life. When she handed me the key, she said, "I wish I could do more, but it's all I have to give you. I might not have much of a Christmas this year."

I thought, *We'll see about that!* I decided to surprise DJ by buying a Christmas tree, presents and decorations. I went to her apartment before she arrived home from work, set up the tree, placed the presents under it and decorated the place. When DJ walked in, she asked, "Did you do all this, Pink?" I nodded my head. She came to me, hugged me and gave me a long lingering kiss. She said, "This is one of the best Christmases I ever had."

"And it's only our first," I replied.

An issue concerning a legal discrepancy came up that required my making a two-week trip to Michigan in January. When I told DJ about this she asked, "Where will you be staying?"

"With my mother and father, and that's another problem. I don't wanna tell anyone in my family about us until the time is right."

"There's not gonna be anything goin' on I should worry about, is there?"

"I give you my word, there won't be."

Being secretive made me uncomfortable because true love speaks the truth, but I was still scared to death she would never accept me after hearing what my life had been before meeting her. While I was away, she became angry when she didn't hear from me. When I returned to Orlando, she said, "You made me so mad when you didn't call. I calmed down when I realized I was upset because I love you so much and it's so hard to be apart from you."

DJ also mentioned she was facing a financial crisis. She explained, "The cost of my divorce wiped me out. I have a townhouse, but had to rent it out to pay the mortgage and live in this apartment. The tenants aren't payin' the rent and I'm behind on the mortgage." Tears welled in her eyes and she sobbed, "I'm gonna lose the place." I asked her, how much was involved and she told me.

Hoping to surprise her, I went to the bank and withdrew some cash. I walked into her apartment with a smile on my face. It felt great knowing

I could solve DJ's problem. I handed her an envelope containing the money and said, "Here, baby, there's enough to get the mortgage caught up."

She wouldn't take the envelope and just stood there shaking her head. She immediately put up her defenses because she still wasn't sure if I was trying to manipulate her. I said, "I want to help you," but it didn't make any difference. She still wouldn't accept the money.

I had to prove my commitment to her, so I purchased a diamond ring and proposed to DJ on Valentine's Day, 1990. I popped the question in her apartment. She was taking a bubble bath, but I was too excited and couldn't wait. I pounded on the bathroom door and said, "DJ, baby, open up! It's an emergency!"

Dripping wet, she opened the door and saw me standing there holding the ring. I said, "DJ, will you marry me? Will you be mine?"

She replied, "Whaat! Really? Oh, Pink! Yes, oh yes." Her words made me the happiest man in the world. I slipped the ring on her finger. We embraced and kissed deeply. No one would ever drive us apart.

I handed her the box the ring came in. A card was attached that read, "To DJ, my one and only true love. I love you with a pink passion."

A month later, my cover was blown when DJ and her mother happened to see a TV newscast about my relocating to Orlando. An Orlando sportscaster proudly announced his city was the new hometown of a former heavyweight champ. Her mother said, "Is that the boy who gave you the ring?'

My beloved replied, "Yes, Mom." Both sat in open mouthed amazement.

DJ was disappointed in me at first for keeping things from her, but we discussed the matter calmly. I said, "I did so many crazy things when I was a kid and while I was fighting. I don't want you to have to deal with any of it. Being with you is starting my life over again. I trust you completely, and you're so good with numbers I want you to handle all my finances."

"Okay, Pink."

"But there's a catch. I want you to go back to school and get your college degree." I had been asking her to do it ever since I visited the juvenile detention facility one night and saw her do a physical takedown of a youth offender. I told her, "This place is too dangerous and it's a waste of time for somebody with your brains." After we had our talk and she agreed to handle my finances, she immediately quit both full time jobs, returned to school and earned her degree. I was very happy for that.

AT THE TOP ONCE MORE

On Good Friday, April thirteenth, 1990, a man of medium height with a broad chest and piercing blue eyes walked into the Howard Johnson gym. He waited until I finished a round of sparring and then introduced himself to Dick Fleming and me. He said, "My name is Dominick Polo, and I'm an agent for George Foreman. I want you to fight him."

Dick asked, "How much of a purse are you offering?"

Polo took out a contract from his briefcase and handed it to Fleming. I looked over my manager's shoulder. The contract was for one and a half million dollars. It would be the largest purse I ever received. Polo took out a pen and offered it to us, saying, "We can wrap this up right now."

Dick replied, "This is pretty sudden. Could you excuse us? I want to talk to Pink for a minute."

My manager took me aside and said, "Pink, let's not appear anxious. We'll tell the guy that we'll discuss it over the weekend and have an answer the Monday after Easter." I agreed that was the best thing to do.

We told Polo we'd have an answer for him on Monday and kept the contract so Dick could go over it. He invited me and DJ to attend Easter services with his family. We drove to the Fleming residence, left our car there and rode in Dick's van, along his wife, Gail, and their five children. Arriving at the church, Dick asked DJ and his wife to take the kids, saying, "We'll be right in." He turned to me and said, "Pink, I have some bad news."

"What is it?"

"Dominick Polo died in his sleep last night."

I laughed because I thought Dick was kidding. The somber look on his face told me he wasn't. Polo, a former U.S. Marine, had suffered a fatal heart attack at the age of fifty-three. Our million-and-a-half-dollar deal died along with him.

The setback didn't deter me from my comeback. I won a ten-round decision over Curtis Isaac, but was upset by Mike Hunter at Fort Bragg, North Carolina in June, 1990. Three months later, I took on unbeaten Riddick Bowe at the University of the District of Columbia Activities Center in our nation's capitol. It would be a ten round bout held in his home base. I had experience on my side, but he had legendary trainer Eddie Futch in his corner. Mentally, I was up to the challenge by a fighter ten years younger, but my body was telling me "No."

Bowe had won eighteen straight with sixteen knockouts, but had never gone more than four rounds, so my strategy was to tire him out and then go for a knockout. The first three rounds were unexpectedly tough for me, and I realized he was getting stronger while I was getting weaker. I knew I would be out of gas after four rounds, so I gave it all I had in the fourth. I landed a series of combinations that stunned the six-foot five-inch Olympic silver medal winner and backed him toward the ropes. Suddenly, potbellied referee Sylvester Stevens came between us and stopped the fight. Stevens said to me, "Tape on one of your gloves came loose."

Both Bowe and I were sent to neutral corners and the political tricks of boxing came into play. There was an inch of loose tape on my left glove and it should have been quickly resolved by wrapping tape once around my wrist. Instead, Stevens insisted tape had to be applied six times. The two-minute delay revived Riddick Bowe, but my tank was almost empty. By the time the fight was stopped in the eighth round and Bowe awarded a TKO, I had no energy left, was staggering around the ring and glad the bout was over. Later that night, I discovered blood in my urine. This caused both DJ and me great concern but fortunately, it didn't lead to a serious health issue.

I didn't fight again until February, 1991 when Jackie Kallen and Dick Fleming arranged for me to face blonde white hope Tommy "Duke" Morrison in Kansas City's Kemper Arena. Tommy was 25 and 0 with 21 knockouts, was a distant relative of iconic John Wayne and had a featured role in Rocky V, which had come out the year before. I weighed in at two twenty-six and a half, two pounds more than my opponent, and was an inch taller than Tommy, but he had an inch and a half longer reach. Seems like everybody I fought had a longer reach than me, except Mike Tyson.

I was not in top shape and unable to get out of the way of Morrison's punches. In the first round, he hit me with a left hook that opened a cut over my right eye so deep it went all the way through the eyebrow. "Tommy the Duke" continued landing painful blows leaving bad bruises and had me on the ropes at the end of the round. I had never been hit so hard, even by Tyson. It was as though I had been slammed repeatedly with a baseball bat. As I sat on the stool in my corner, I told my handlers, "I'm through." The fight was stopped and Tommy Morrison was awarded a TKO.

Upon entering my dressing room, I was surprised to find a plastic surgeon ready to skillfully apply eighteen stitches to my wound in a way that would prevent a scar. DJ said, "Honey, I was scared you were gonna be disfigured. How was that man able to hit you so hard?" In months to come, I heard from several credible sources that Tommy Morrison's gloves had been loaded. There was no way to follow up on this because neither Kansas City nor the state of Missouri had a boxing commission. Once again, I had been set up.

After losing to Morrison, I decided to call a halt to my boxing career. I had recovered from my addiction and continued running, training and working out to assure I remained sober. DJ couldn't imagine me fighting anymore after losing my last three bouts. A year went by and I was in the best shape I'd been in years. Prizefighting was still in my blood, a sour taste remained from the Morrison bout and I didn't want my career to end with that fight. I had unfinished business and decided to step into the ring again. DJ didn't want me to fight anymore, so I kept the true purpose of my training secret

I finally told her what was going on two fights after embarking on a comeback. I had a guilty conscience and didn't want her to find out through television, like she did the first time.

My comeback went amazingly well and I won twelve in a row. The bouts took place in the Carolinas, Virginia, Alabama and Florida. Some of the venues were very small. One fight card was held in a North Carolina bingo parlor with a ceiling so low, my head bumped against it. Ceiling tiles had to be removed before my fight could start.

Twelve victories in five months of living out of a motor home brought me a title shot on November fourteenth, 1992 in Greenville, South Carolina. At stake was the first International Boxing Organization World Heavyweight Championship. Craig Payne from Apopka, Florida was my opponent for the scheduled twelve rounds. His claims to fame were fighting Teofilo Stevenson, three-time Olympic gold medalist from Cuba, being part of George Foreman's training camp and winning an amateur bout with Mike Tyson. Dick Fleming warned, "The guy is tough. He gave Tyson such a whipping Iron Mike will never fight him as a pro." Payne was in superb condition. He weighed in at two hundred eighty-nine pounds and I figured he would be two ninety six when we were in the ring.

At the start of our championship bout, I foolishly tried to go toe to toe with him. I discovered the large economy sized boxer packed a punch like a nuclear bomb. He also possessed amazing stamina for someone so big and similar to George Foreman, he never sat down between rounds. I began to get worried after the sixth round. At the end of twelve rounds, the decision was split among the judges and I was awarded the first IBO heavyweight title. Since it was a new title, my purse was much lower than usual, but winning a second world championship was a priceless moment.

The championship also opened the door to an opportunity I had coveted for years... a chance to get in the ring with Larry Holmes. The man who had ducked me for so long contacted Dick Fleming and said, "If Pink wins the vacant WBF title, I'll fight him." Holmes indicated my purse would be well over a million, the biggest I ever had. I felt that time was running out on my clock and pressed Dick to set up a fight for the WBF belt. It was scheduled for January twenty third, 1993. I would be facing Lawrence "Poncho" Carter in Columbia, South Carolina.

It was a mistake to take a fight less than two months after winning the IBO title. The wise thing would have been to take six months off and not be so consumed with the idea of getting a million-dollar purse to fight Larry Holmes. Holmes had become my personal Moby Dick, and we all know what happened to Captain Ahab in that story. I didn't tell anyone about blinding headaches I suffered every day after my fight with huge heavyweight Craig Payne. I also made a big mistake of doing roadwork in heavy work boots laced up to the top that ruined my knees and limited my mobility. These wrongheaded decisions left me with as little chance of winning as a duck trying to pull a truck.

DJ was at ringside, and it was the first time she attended any of my fights in over a year and a half. By this time, we had two daughters; Peyton and Pierra. Pierra was just an infant, while Peyton was pre-kindergarten age, but unusually mature for someone so young. She and I were inseparable. She was the most amazing child I'd ever known and I adored her. At the age of two, Peyton ate with a knife and fork, had impeccable manners and spoke with perfect diction. Both our little girls were at the fight, and DJ's cousin, Paulette, had come along to help with our daughters. My wife wouldn't let just anyone watch her children, but Paulette had served in the Army and DJ trusted her completely.

Paulette was holding Pierra while DJ was taking care of Peyton. Just before the championship fight began, Peyton had to go to the bathroom and my wife got up to take her there. The bout went on while they were in the restroom.

My thirty-four-year-old legs were gone in the sixth round, and my feet felt like they were encased in cement blocks, I was unable to defend myself and was knocked unconscious by Carter in the seventh. Poncho was not what I would call a hard hitter, but a perfect storm of mistakes made while training did me in.

Paulette had never seen a boxing match before and the sight of paramedics rushing into the ring, then failing to revive me was more than she could bear. She feared I had gone to My Maker and became physically ill. Her chest tightened, she was sweating profusely and found it hard to catch her breath. She needed to go to the bathroom and didn't know if she could make it there in time. Noticing a black woman in an Army uniform with sergeant's stripes, she asked the woman to hold Pierra while she went to the restroom.

When Paulette walked into the ladies room, DJ saw her cousin was perspiring heavily. She asked her, "Paulette, what's wrong!"

"I gotta go to the bathroom." Paulette was drenched in perspiration.

"Where's my baby?"

"I gave her to a black woman who's a sergeant in the Army."

"*Whaaat?*"

"Something happened to Pink. I feel sick." After getting those words out, Paulette collapsed. I was unconscious, DJ's cousin was unconscious and Pierra was lost.

While paramedics worked to revive Paulette and I was transported to Baptist Medical Center, DJ had everyone in my entourage looking for our infant daughter. After two hours of searching, Dick Fleming's daughter, Sarah, found the Army sergeant holding Pierra. The sergeant would not allow Sarah to take the baby, saying, "I'm not turning the child over to anyone but her mother. She won't have to say a word. I can tell who she is by looking at her." When she was brought to DJ, she exclaimed, "That's the baby's mother, no doubt about it!" Our precious two-month nine-day-old baby girl was safe in her mother's arms

Arriving at the hospital, DJ was told I had suffered a subdural hematoma and there was bleeding in my brain. The hospital staff awaited a neurosurgeon being flown in. Surgery would be performed at nine in the morning if the bleeding hadn't subsided. Two holes would be drilled in my head and shunts placed in my brain to allow blood to drain evenly and relieve pressure. When I was examined the next morning, the doctors discovered the bleeding had stopped, praise be to God.

I didn't awaken for two days. After regaining consciousness, I was still not completely out of my mental fog. I needed to go to the bathroom and stumbled out of bed. DJ tried to help me, but my equilibrium was still not what it should have been and I fell on top of her. She couldn't move my dead weight, and male nurses had to lift me from her.

Once I was back to my normal state of mind, I faced a brow furrowing crisis about my future and the futures of DJ and the children. I had compiled a boxing record of forty-three wins, seven losses and a draw and won two world titles, but could no longer take on any bouts. How was I to earn a living? Boxing was all I'd ever known, and I could no longer be a fighter. The sands of time were running low for me.

DJ was at my bedside when I brought up a serious topic. I said, "Baby, I'm gonna give you some money. I want you to take the kids and start a new life. I don't have a way of makin' a living anymore. I can't provide for you and them. You're a young woman, and I don't want you burdened with me."

She took my hands in hers, looked through my eyes into my heart and soul and replied, "Pink, I don't care if you have to pick apples or pump gas. We're gonna get through this together."

"You really wanna stay with me, D.J.?"

"I defy anyone to try and separate us. True love came to us, and we can solve anything together."

Our hearts were as one, and we were both willing to sacrifice. I loved her so much I was willing to lose her if it would mean her future happiness, but she loved me so much she was willing to stay with a man who didn't seem to have much of a future.

"By the way," she said, "I already contacted your father and your family and told them you're gonna be okay." My parents knew I fought that night and didn't receive a call from me, like they normally did after any of my bouts. They were deeply worried until DJ called them. She said, "It was the hardest thing I ever had to do. I was very concerned about how your mother, with her health issues, would handle being told of your misfortune. But she sounded relieved when I told her you were getting the best of care." It was great that DJ eased their minds. She added, "All you need to worry about is getting better."

When I was released after four days, Paulette took our children home by car. DJ purchased two airline tickets for us because I was in such a critical state she didn't want to risk returning by train and having something go wrong.

I recovered completely from my injury and my addictions, thanks in no small part to DJ, my daughters and grandchildren. They are the apples of my eye, and I'm very protective of them. Peyton is a polished lady with impeccable manners. Both PaQuana and Pierra followed my athletic path. Both competed in track and PaQuana participated in karate, while Pierra took part in weightlifting. DJ and PaQuana have an uncanny relationship. My wife said to me, "The moment we first met, we instantly recognized each other. It's as if I gave birth to her."

I said in response, "It was meant to be."

I also find great pleasure in my pets. I grew up with dogs, and the furry, snuggly creatures with gum drop eyes have always been an important part of my life. They are instant mood boosters. No matter how rough a day I had, the sight of them joyfully wagging their tails or rolling over for belly rubs put a smile on my face and lifted my spirits. All my canine companions have been unselfish and showed unconditional love for me. They also reminded me God is the creator of all things great and small. By treating my pets with kindness and affection and taking care of them to the best of my ability, I honor Him. God, in His divine wisdom, knew I would need both people and animals in my life in order to feel close to Him.

I learned the hard way only God could mend my life. Once I learned this truth, I accepted Jesus Christ as my Personal Savior and placed my life in the hands of The Lord. The Word of God both guides and guards my life. I trust God in every circumstance and can give thanks to Him even in times of misfortune. I rejoice always, pray continuously and give thanks constantly.

I came from a chaotic past, but was able to face a challenging future with enthusiasm, patience and persistence because I'm fortunate to be married to the greatest woman in the world. For me to have found her is a miracle. With DJ's help and the Grace of God, I was able to come all the way back from the edge of Hell.

*"We have to keep our children away
from getting started into drugs and alcohol
and provide the support, guidance and love they need."*

BRINGING OUT THE GOOD IN OUR YOUNG

While recuperating from my head injury, I asked God to help me make a living with my gift of gab, since I could no longer do so with my fists. My Lord and Master answered my prayer by calling upon me to share the wisdom gained through experiences that nearly finished me off and bring hope to troubled youth and those struggling along the road to sobriety.

With the wholehearted support of my wife, I started on my quest by working with a teenage boy in our neighborhood. Fifteen-year-old Bryan Crenshaw began training with me in a gym I had set up in my garage. He was very close to his little sister, Jenny, who died tragically when a dentist overdosed her with anesthesia. It was a sensational case covered on national television. The loss of his sister was so painful he could never talk about it. He dropped out of school, but his mother intervened. She knew the owner of a teen night club and he hired the boy, who proved to be a dependable and hard-working employee.

After a year of my training him, Bryan was six foot three, a hundred ninety pounds and showed potential as a heavyweight. He introduced his friend, Rocco Gaglioti to me, and the six-foot five-inch fifteen-year-old joined in with us. My new pupil already had some experience with combat sports, having competed in Junior Olympic tae kwon do at fourteen. His mother was born deaf, and the boy became fluent in Italian and excellent at communicating in sign language. Both boys worked hard learning how to box.

One night, I received a frantic phone call from DJ, who was on her way home. She said, "Pink, the police have Bryan and Rocco! They're just down the street from us."

I bolted from the house wearing only Nikes, sweat pants and a tank top. I saw Bryan's car and as I came closer to it, I could see the police had both boys lying face down on the ground. The police officers knew me and to my shock, told me Bryan and Rocco were involved with a gang. I assured the officers I would get to the bottom of it, and they released the teenagers to me.

I put them in my car, drove to Bryan's house and knocked on the front door. When Barbara Crenshaw answered, she saw her son and his friend with faces as white as sheets. I had the boys sit in living room chairs, while Mrs. Crenshaw sat in a dining room chair and I stood as I spoke to them.

The two teenagers were mortified, and I came at them hard, saying, "You two think you're tough! Ya wanna be in a gang? Lemme tell ya what it's like bein' in a gang. I'll tell ya about the Black Disciples. It's a mean, nasty way of existing. They'll take advantage of what they can get from ya, then throw ya under a bus." I spoke for a half hour, telling them all about my days as a teenage addict and armed robber. At the end I said, "If ya wanna be in a gang, chances are you'll end up in prison or dead. Ya wanna rot in a cell 'til ya love the walls? Ya wanna give your mothers funerals to go to?" All the while, tears were rolling down Barbara's face.

After hearing my story, the boys thought I was done, but I surprised them. I took Bryan and Rocco to my garage, saying, "We're gonna see how tough ya are. Ya wanna fight somebody, ya can fight me." By now, they were both angry and leaped at a chance to hit me. We all put on gloves and Bryan went first. I landed a punch to his nose and blood poured out like water from a fountain.

DJ tended to him and was able to stop the bleeding. Seeing what happened to his older friend, Rocco declined to battle with me.

The tough love administered that night turned their lives around. They admitted to me there were handguns and other weapons in Bryan's car and they were planning to engage a rival gang. From that point forward, neither had any more to do with gangs or anything else that would disappoint me. After breaking them down, they continued following my guidance and I was able to build them up.

At seventeen, Rocco earned a black belt in karate and was spotted by a talent scout for a modeling agency. It led to a career as a producer of a television series and a documentary on fashion. Bryan also went into entertainment; managing a nightclub at eighteen, running security teams for big rave events, creating Cloud Nine, Orlando's version of New York's legendary Studio 54. The high school dropout displayed amazing creativity and brought the central Florida city a rave scene to equal Miami and the Big Apple. Having finally earned his GED at the age of thirty-nine, Bryan is currently a web designer based in San Antonio, Texas. He's happily married with six kids, four dogs and three horses. I'm very proud of how both Bryan and Rocco turned their lives around and would love to spend the rest of my life helping other young people do the same.

Learning of the two boys' involvement with a gang made me stop and think about the enormous sums street gangs took in from peddling crack cocaine. No wonder they were expanding their operations into other parts of the nation, and Florida was ripe for plucking, The Crips and Bloods from Los Angeles, New York City's Latin Kings and the Disciples from the Midwest all found fertile ground in Orlando. Feeling guilty for having helped these criminal enterprises by spending hundreds of thousands for poison to put in my system, I became determined to keep as many young people as I could from having their souls scarred by predatory gangbangers. My experiences gave me a calling.

I thought about "taking my rumble to the streets" by starting a Pinklon Thomas Anti-Crime and Anti-Drug Program. Testing the waters, I discussed the idea with Tom Teleky, the chiropractor who served as my cut man. He said, "It's a fantastic idea, Pink. In addition to boxing skills, you can teach kids about life by example. The fact that you personally experienced how drugs have a negative effect on a young man's life will let the kids know you're for real, and they'll accept you."

I asked Tom, "What else should the program include?"

He replied, "You should bring up that there's a correlation between poor children, poor health and poor learning. Superior teaching is of little benefit to a child who's physically incapable of learning. Far too many economically deprived youth are leading unhealthy lives and are not physically fit."

I then reached out to Anthony Triano with the Parkside Lodge of Orlando. He had a decade of experience in substance abuse treatment, mainly with young people caught up in the legal system. We put together an outline for a program to combat drugs and crime. It would offer young people an opportunity to train and become members of an Orlando based amateur boxing team, network to find help for those with substance abuse issues, conduct physical examinations, find help for those with medical needs, offer encouragement to continue or return to school and establish a network for job training and placement.

With Tom and Anthony's encouragement, I visited local civic leaders. Chief of Police Danny Wilson welcomed me, saying, "Your idea is just what's needed but unfortunately, there's a shortage of such programs. I wish you luck in your endeavor." State Senator Richard Crotty thanked me for visiting his office and said, "Your program is certainly a worthy one." Mayor Bill Frederick greeted me by saying, "Drugs are pervasive in our community, and we're looking for innovative ways to combat them. Your concept is just that!"

The supportive words from those in positions of authority assured me I was on the right track, but the journey had just begun. What I envisioned involved sports, education, healthcare and economic factors. It was a huge undertaking requiring resources, and I was one man trying to lift an enormous project off the ground. Deep within me, I knew it would all come together somehow.

The Gateway School, a facility for students requiring special instruction, asked me to deliver a motivational speech for their "Day of Sharing." In my presentation, I encouraged the students to believe in themselves and strive to accomplish greatness. I told them, "Don't fold up when you face a setback. Adapt, and then finish what you start. No matter the distance, show persistence." The speech was well received and one of the teachers asked me to visit her class of girls the next day.

The young ladies were leery of me at first but by avoiding talking down to them and being willing to answer all their questions, I won them over. The advice I gave them included, "When you get older, you'll grow a little bolder, but you'll hafta handle a bigger boulder on your shoulder. Hopefully by then, fire and ambition will start to smolder in your eyes. Get your minds set to be the best. It won't be easy and there'll be stress. But what's the point of goin' for it if there's no test? So grab greatness and attach your name to it." I closed with, "That's all for now, but I'll be back later to share more wisdom and scare off haters." They appreciated not being preached to and thanked me for teaching them some "good stuff."

Word of my appearances at the Gateway School reached Walter Hawkins, who headed a black coalition fighting drugs and crime in Orlando. He contacted me in April, 1993 and said, "Pink, I know of a job that would be a great fit for you." On his recommendation, I applied for the position of adolescent behavioral and substance abuse counselor with the Center for Drug Free Living. The organization was planning to broaden their scope of activities by opening a combination school and custodial facility for convicted male youth offenders.

I was interviewed by a panel of seven men seated at a large table with a grandfather clock immediately behind the one asking questions. Wanting to make my best impression, I dressed in a suit and brought along both my championship belts.

They offered me a chair across from the man directing the interview, and I began talking at nine in the morning. My opening words were, "There are too many kids who feel the drug scene is the only way for them. I'm specially qualified to work with them because of my childhood background, my success as a boxer, my personal involvement with drugs and my recovery. I was in a slump, pulled myself out of a dump and can take my rumble to the streets."

Twenty minutes later, none of the seven men had said a word and I continued making a presentation. Nine-forty came, and I had not been asked any questions or told to stop. I continued telling my life story, while the men leaned on their elbows without a word. I began to worry I had lost their attention and they weren't going to hire me.

My stomach began to churn at the thought of losing out on a chance at what I knew in my heart was my calling. Noticing some bored expressions, I thought, *They gonna kick me outta the room.* I decided to keep talking and not let any of them get a word in edgewise.

A quote from World Featherweight Champ and Hall of Famer Willie Pep flashed in my mind. *I'm all right until I hear a bell. That's when I go off.* I looked at the grandfather clock going tic-tic-tic and saw it was nine fifty-nine. At ten, the big clock struck ten times and on the third "ding," I jumped from my chair, started looking around and began laughing. The man leading the interview asked, "What's wrong?"

I replied, "I'm all right until I hear a bell. That's when I go off."

The seven men found the remark hilarious and laughed so hard, they held their sides and gasped for breath. The leader said, "Okay, okay, Mr. Thomas, that's cool. We're going to step outside for a moment." They left me alone in the room and when they returned ten minutes later, I was hired on the spot.

I was part of the original staff when the twelve-thousand-acre Adolescent Residential Campus opened in Poinciana, Florida during May, 1993. We were placed in charge of ninety-six males between the ages of thirteen and nineteen. Those turning eighteen while in the juvenile justice system were held until they were nineteen. The young men came from various counties within the state and included multiple races and ethnic groups. They had been convicted of offenses ranging from drug charges, weapons charges to carjacking, and even included home invasion and rape. Products of single parent, drug infested households, they grew up in a world where positive male role models were rare. These youngsters disrespected women and had no respect for anyone, including themselves.

The young men were referred to as "clients" and classified as either Level Six or Level Eight youth offenders. Level Six offenders were sentenced to the campus for six months, while sentences for Level Eight offenders ranged from eight months to a year and a half. They attended classes leading to a GED, and some received training in culinary arts from a stellar chef. Client housing consisted of four cottages, two for Level Eight offenders and two for Level Six. Each accommodated twenty-four and was named for a species of animal. Level Eight was housed in the Buffalo and Antelope cottages, while Level Six was in the Cougar and Dolphin cottages. All residents wore t-shirts color coded to the cottages they were assigned. Level Eight cottages ate their meals at different times from Level Six, and cottages were kept separate while in the dining area.

A twenty-foot-high chain link fence topped with three feet of barbed wire, surrounded the campus. None of the staff were armed, but we were all issued walkie talkies for maintaining contact with each other or calling for assistance from the local sheriff's department.

Clients weren't allowed to walk anywhere unless escorted by two staff members; one alongside and one in back. Visitation was every Saturday. All clients' mail was opened, read and censored. Phone privileges consisted of two calls a week lasting no longer than fifteen minutes a call. The calls were monitored and a staff member had to dial the number for the client. In addition to alcohol and cigarettes, coins or paper money were considered contraband. The clients were permitted to have money on the books for making purchases at a commissary with a very limited selection. Each cottage had a radio and a television, but use of those devices was restricted.

Any rules breaking resulted in a behavior report being filed, and a client who became a chronic trouble maker could have time added to their sentence. Rodney, a sixteen-year-old who was one of the first clients brought to the campus, had twenty two reports written on him in one day. When asked why he kept rebelling against authority, his answer was, "If I wasn't doin' this, would you care I existed?" Like all the clients, Rodney's life had been caught up in negativity. He had been repeatedly told, "There's no way out and your dreams are impossible."

In the beginning, the clients were punished for doing something wrong, but never rewarded for good behavior. Kids need to hear things that promote self esteem and hope, so I decided to put together programs promoting positivity and peace.

Our first group of clients had been sent to us from the lockup of a juvenile detention center. They tried to impress the staff with how mean and tough they were, but their edginess didn't play well. Their wild, unruly hair appeared not to have been shampooed or even combed. Their pants sagged so low they were almost on the ground and their underwear was showing. The older ones sported scraggly beards. Looking at the shabby group, I remembered what Bob Kaiser had said so many times. "No matter the crime, the child is still mine." I had committed to help make men out of miscreants and quickly instituted a dress code.

I ordered, "Pull your trousers up and tuck in your shirts. We don't allow pants on the ground here." After all of them complied, I said, "Now that your trousers are up and shirts tucked in, stand with your head and eyes straight ahead and arms at your sides. Look people in the eye. If you're told to sit, sit correctly. No slouching. If you're told to stand, stand tall." Later that day, the beards were cut off and each client's head shaved bald. It reminded me of the time Momma shaved off all my hair when I was caught using stolen hair straightening solution.

Mistakes were made in setting up the cafeteria by placing salt and pepper shakers on the tables and distributing metal eating utensils. Several fights broke out and the shakers were used as brass knuckles and knives, forks and spoons became shanks. I suggested packets of sugar and salt, as well as much less dangerous plastic utensils, be used. When I interviewed clients about the cause of the fights, they admitted some fighting was along gang or racial lines, but much of it happened out of boredom.

It wasn't long before the first escape attempt took place. Two clients stole a staff car and rammed through the gate. Others attempted to climb the wire fence or dash out the gate whenever it was opened. None of the escapees were at large for long. When brought back, their shoes were taken, forcing them to walk around in socks and flip flops, and they were given special colored uniforms to wear.

I believed if the clients had less time on their hands, there would be less fights and escape attempts. The first step to keeping the clients occupied was holding morning meetings. Rather than allow them to mill around outside their cottages while waiting to go to breakfast, I had the clients all line up in front of the flagpole in the center of the campus. I would begin by saying, "Good morning." Ninety-six male teenagers replied in one nice loud voice, "Good morning."

At the first morning meeting I announced, "Man begins to achieve when he begins to believe. That's your Tone for the Day. Startin' tomorrow morning, each cottage will come up with a Tone. At the end of the week, the best Tone gets an award. At the end of the month, the cottage with the most awards gets a five-star gourmet meal."

The contest generated enthusiasm and the clients avidly spent their free time searching the Holy Bible and other books for inspirational sayings. A Level Six cottage won the first gourmet meal with the prizewinning Tone "Green ideas sleep furiously, like seeds waiting to sprout into beautiful trees." The feast was prepared by the culinary arts class, served in a large meeting room on the campus and came complete with chafing dishes. The Tone Contest was later expanded to include a Talent Contest, with the choice of a gourmet meal or barbeque as first prize. The contests made the clients aware of how much more could be accomplished by working together, rather than everyone for themselves.

I also instituted a physical conditioning program and organized athletic leagues. The purpose was not only to get the clients in shape, keep them in shape and burn pent up energy. I felt athletic competition was important because through games, young people learn to cope with life, acquire an ability to work, learn to cooperate with others and sharpen cognitive skills by mastering required fundamentals and learning the rules.

I would go to each cottage and ask, "Who wants to come out for physical conditioning?" Usually a total of eighteen from the four cottages participated. At first, I accompanied them on long runs through the campus and performed exercises with them. I decided to broaden the program by making use of a basketball gym on campus. It had originally been equipped with free weights, but they had been removed after all the fights when the campus first opened.

The gym could be used for basketball and volleyball, and I also found a heavy bag and a speed bag that had been stored away. With the help of some of the clients, the bags were set up and I began teaching them how to box. I also formed basketball and volleyball leagues. Many clients possessed amazing athletic ability and as the weeks went by, there were far less fights and escape attempts and the athletic competition on campus became more popular than TV shows.

Knowing the clients would have to return to neighborhoods and negative atmospheres that led them into trouble, I also used the time in the gym and on the playing fields as an opportunity to teach life skills. I told the clients "You're third world citizens. I'm gonna prepare you for real life and get you ready to get outta here. You'll be able to go right into what you need to do, but it's not gonna be easy. You'll have to work harder than the ones you'll be competin' with. You been locked up, incarcerated and already earned a bad name. You'll carry that record with you the rest of your life and you'll hafta work three times as hard as anyone else, but ya can do it. Don't let the past dictate who ya are. Let it be a lesson that strengthens the person you'll become. You wanna be the best, you gotta work harder than the rest. Remember, it's deeds, not words, that matter most. I been to the mountain top, heard others talk big and seen 'em drop."

The vast majority of our clients never had a male mentor in their life, a crutch to clutch on their free fall through existence and adversity. I tried to fill that void, hoping to end their generational cycles of poverty, fear, violence, injury and death. In hopes of encouraging them to set realistic, achievable goals and not be afraid to dream, I often shared lessons with them. "Don't be afraid to speak up if you know the answer, and don't be afraid to admit you don't know the answer. Admittin' you don't know somethin' is the first step to learnin' somethin' new. Don't hold yourself back. Anything's possible if ya tear down the wall between dreams and reality. All it takes is blood, sweat and tears." I also planned activities, such as movie and popcorn sessions, that offered additional opportunities to share lessons. Films the clients were shown included Cooley High and Hoop Dreams.

What I wanted most of all was to stage an activity bringing together the clients and the entire staff, I came up with the idea of Fun Day and spent three weeks preparing for it. Everyone participated, including maintenance, teachers, counselors, program managers and case managers. Barbeque was prepared for the entire campus. The day began for me at five in the morning, cutting up all the meat and cleaning it. The culinary arts teacher and his students started barbequing at six thirty, and the entire meal was ready by eleven. Fun Games began at five minutes before noon.

I opened the festivities by announcing, "Let the Fun Day begin!" Each cottage was represented by clients wearing the cottage's colors. The first events were the mile run, the fifty-yard dash, the two twenty, the four forty relay and a volleyball competition. After volleyball, barbeque was served and the kids relaxed for an hour before I had them work off their calories by participating in tug of wars and jumping jacks.

Two cottages tied for number of events won, so the top two competed in a tiebreaker called a "Pinkathon." Each client from those cottages had to do a hundred sit ups, a hundred pushups, a hundred up and downs and a hundred squats and the cottage completing the exercises first was the winner. The Pinkathon generated huge enthusiasm. Staff members were on their feet, cheering kids giving their all for those they shared a cottage with. Shouts of, "YOU CAN DO IT! COME ON, YOU CAN DO IT!" echoed throughout the campus. At the end, all contestants shook hands. It was sportsmanship at its finest, and I felt tremendous elation at having brought everyone together, at least for an afternoon.

The success of the Adolescent Residential Campus led to additional opportunities for me to help improve the destinies of troubled youth. The Center for Drug Free Living opened an Adolescent Therapeutic Center for young people with diagnosed psychiatric difficulties. I served as a counselor at that facility, assisting with intense intervention and treatment.

The Center for Drug Free Living broadened their horizon even more with a Midnight Basketball program that drew national acclaim. I managed one of four sites where on Friday and Saturday nights, from nine until one in the morning, at risk youth built self-esteem, sharpened their basketball skills and enhanced their physical condition. They competed in either of two classifications: Fifteen years of age and younger or sixteen and older. After two games were played in each division, I would announce to the players, "Hit the wall! It's Topic Time."

After they were all lined up against a wall, I would deliver a brief talk about achieving success. One of my talks began, "What you think about is what you become, and the best part is you can decide what you think about. You'll do better if you think about what you want, instead of what you don't want. It's better to think about what makes you excited than what you don't want to happen. Dreams and goals are what should be on your mind.

"Don't follow the crowd. Spend more time in books than in the streets or instant gratification will take over your mind like a snake wrapped like a vine around a tree. Choose a path and tread it. And don't get caught up in grudges that let somebody live in your head rent free. Just remember, the choices you make when you're young are crucial to your future success." I was constantly trying to get their heads wrapped around the idea that deep inside, they were good persons who needed to find something so important to them it would drive them to succeed.

More than twenty years have gone by since I became a counselor, but I'm still surprised by men who went through one of the Center for Drug Free Living's programs and unexpectedly approach me in restaurants or convenience stores. They thank me for encouraging them to face reality, tell the truth and use their ability to reason. Putting their troubled youths behind them, they are now happily married and proud fathers with bright futures and nothing but opportunities in front of them.

It's exhilarating to be recognized as a mentor who made a difference by helping a kid get back on the right path and turn their life around. I was once a lost soul headed for doom, but, God, in His eternal mercy, allowed me a chance to have my testimony of survival and redemption change lives for the better.

My work is not over, and I continue "taking my rumble to the streets" by telling my story to kids, as well as adults, at neighborhood centers, churches, sporting events, celebrity golf tournaments, schools and juvenile facilities. I also designed Project P.I.N.K. (Pride In Neighborhood Kids) which offers activities and opportunities to teach skills, give guidance and assist in balancing the lives of young people. All of this was possible only through the Grace of God.

TIME MARCHES ON

I am so grateful for the blessings God, in His wisdom, granted me. They include my wonderful wife and my children. I'm very proud of my daughters and my son. PaQuana lives in Pontiac and works as a manager for an established firm. Peyton is employed full time with the Government and has a Bachelor's degree in Accounting. Pierra earned a degree in Health Sciences from University of Central Florida and also has an RN Degree from Valencia College, and is working for a major hospital. She's holding down a full-time job, while also pursuing a modeling career. My son, Pinklon III, works as a personal trainer in Chicago.

I've made many friends through boxing. The most colorful was Hector "Macho" Camacho. During the world title fight with Tim Witherspoon, I noticed Hector cheering on my opponent. I had seen Camacho fight several times and thought he was a dynamic mixture of energy, talent and raw nerve. He fought his way out of the mean streets of Spanish Harlem and became a world champion. As time went on, Hector and I became very close friends, sometimes trained in the same gym and often appeared on the same covers of boxing magazines. Four years younger than me, I became a big brother to him. He was a delight to be around, always dancing and doing things which brought a smile to my face and brightened my day. His very presence completely changed the atmosphere of any room he was in.

Both of us were left-handed, but I fought in a right-hand stance, while he boxed as a southpaw. I never saw anyone move their arms as fast as Hector. He was speed in its purest form and won three world championships in three different weight divisions; Super featherweight, lightweight and junior welterweight. With his crazy spit curl, outrageous costumes worn when entering the ring and wildly designed boxing trunks, the Macho Man was an unforgettable athlete who took ring entertainment to another level. Some described him as arrogant, but I thought of him as having an amazing amount of self confidence.

Hector and I once happened to be on the same plane to Detroit. He was headed there to purchase a Chrysler Crossfire direct from the factory and DJ and I were going to Pontiac for a visit with my dad. We mentioned it to Hector and he said he'd like to meet my father. After transacting his business, he drove his brand-new sports coupe to Pontiac. My mom was no longer alive, but Hector was so excited with his new car that an aura of energy engulfed me, my wife, my dad and everyone else at the family barbeque, making the festive gathering even more fun filled. He loved being with people, and enjoyed sharing his popularity with his birthplace of Bayamon, Puerto Rico and hometown of Harlem.

Hector's life ended far too soon during Thanksgiving weekend, 2012. He was in the wrong place at the wrong time and fell victim to a drive by shooting. I was interviewed by reporters for three days straight. I tried to hold it together, but my sorrow got the better of me and I broke down while on camera. Hector left us at the age of fifty, and I will always miss him. He is remembered as a boxer, a showman and a champion.

God's help in achieving sobriety led to amazing chapters in my life, but those years were not trouble free. I suffered health setbacks because of Hepatitis C. I was first diagnosed with it in 1997, in the course of taking an insurance physical. Doctors told me I initially contracted the virus decades before from intravenous drug use. It lay dormant from my teenage years until I was thirty-nine and the viral load was large enough to be detected. My physician countered it by administering weekly injections of Interferon for twenty-two months, which brought the viral load down from millions to a number posing no threat. Hepatitis C flared up again in 2012. This time, I was given Harvoni, manufactured by Gilead Sciences. After taking a Harvoni pill each day for two and a half months, my viral load was undetectable. Since then, I've had no further problems with Hepatitis C, thanks to God, the Master Builder.

Both my parents suffered from cancer, making it inevitable I would also be afflicted. I was diagnosed with prostate cancer on December thirteenth, 2014. It was the start of a very tough month. My father passed away on December twenty third at the age of one hundred and was buried in Pontiac on December thirtieth. After returning from Michigan, I began my treatment on January second, 2015. Thanks to God's mercy, my physicians caught it in time. Since then, there's been no recurrence. I truly believe the decades of my being vigilant about my addiction prepared me for battling my health issues. To date I have had over fifteen major surgeries, some of them were life threatening.

As a cancer stomping survivor, I learned the best thing that can be done for anyone suffering from the disease is treat them as if they're still the same as they were before and make sincere offers to help out. It means so much for them to hear, "If there's anything I can do, let me know." Above all, when you're around them, act as though there's nothing out of the ordinary. Nobody wants to be a pity case. Little things mean a lot, and warmth, sincerity and genuine concern are very therapeutic.

The best advice I can pass along to cancer patients is, "Don't let your illness make you afraid to live the rest of your life. Make each day productive and enjoy it to the fullest." I'm always looking for God's hand in whatever I do. I know He led me to where I am so I might get closer to Him. When going through my bouts with Hepatitis C and cancer, I rejoiced in the relationship Our Heavenly Father was trying to have with me. When God places you in the belly of the whale, as He did to Jonah and to me, it was a sign He will use whatever means necessary to get your attention. Thank goodness He chose to pursue me and not forsake me.

My purpose in writing this book is to make those who find themselves in seemingly hopeless situations realize they should never give up, no matter what happens. Likewise, those battling an illness should never give up until God counts to ten, rings the bell and declares the fight over. Even if you're told by the greatest medical minds in the world you are terminal, it isn't the end of the game. Only Our Maker should decide when that happens.

With the help of God, I achieved full recovery from all my health issues. I'm able to lead an active lifestyle which includes rigorous workouts on a regular basis and training those willing to learn how to box. To show my gratitude for the many ways the Lord has blessed me, I intend to devote the rest of my years helping troubled persons of all ages effect positive changes in their lives, so they may become closer to Him. This may be a task that can't be completed in a single lifetime, but I'm committed to it.

I have been to the edge of Hell and wouldn't wish it on my worst enemy. When your days are spent, it's too late to repent. Right living may mean doing things which seem difficult, tedious, inconvenient or boring, but it is much easier to live right and avoid the fury of Hell than attempt a comeback from eternal damnation.

~ The End ~